Moral, But No Compass

Moral, But No Compass
Government, Church and the Future of Welfare

Francis Davis, Elizabeth Paulhus, Andrew Bradstock

**Von Hügel Institute,
St Edmund's College, Cambridge**

**A Report for the Church of England
commissioned by Rt Rev Stephen Lowe,
Bishop for Urban Life and Faith.**

Matthew James Publishing Ltd

First published in Great Britain 2008 by:
Matthew James Publishing Ltd
19 Wellington Close,
Chelmsford,
Essex CM1 2EE
www.matthew-james.co.uk

ISBN 978-1-898366-91-1
© 2008 The Von Hügel Institute
The moral rights of the authors have been asserted

Further information regarding the work of the Von Hügel Institute is available from:
The Von Hügel Institute
St Edmund's College,
Cambridge, CB3 0BN
www.vhi.org.uk

Design and typesetting by Michael Shaw
Cover design by Gill England

Printed in England, by Cromwell Press

Contents:

Foreword   7
Acknowledgements   9
About the Authors   12
Introduction   13

Part One: Methodology   14
　1.1 Our Brief: A Report for Church and Nation   14
　1.2 The Research Questions   15
　1.3 The Research Process and Methods   16
　1.4 Research Factors   18
　　1.4.1 Congregations or Institutions?   18
　　1.4.2 Social Capital and the Omission of Capability   19
　　1.4.3 The Church's Clash of Self-Perceptions   21
　　1.4.4 Challenges to the Church's Perception   24
　　1.4.5 Social Voices and Representation   26

Part Two: From Past to Present:
　The Development of Modern Welfare Organisation   28
　2.1 The Historical Context   28
　2.2 Current Stances on Public Service Reform   36
　　2.2.1 Labour – Exit, Voice, and Loyalty   36
　　　- Human Rights and the Invasion of Civil Society   38
　　2.2.2 Conservatives – Towards 'A Responsible Society'   39
　　2.2.3 In Sum   42
　2.3 Are All 'Contracts' the Same?   43
　　　- Best Practice and the Dangers of 'Service on the Cheap'   46
　2.4 The Risk of Self-Referential Radicalism   46
　2.5 A Crisis of Government Evidence and Conversation   48
　2.6 Problems at the Charity Commission and Beyond   50

Part Three: Capability and Structure: Towards an Evidence Base   57
　3.1 Diocesan Survey   57
　　3.1.1 Financial Resources   57
　　3.1.2 Human Resources   59
　　3.1.3 Surveys, in Sum   64
　3.2 Cathedrals: Regional Power Houses in Local Communities   65
　3.3 Bishops   69
　3.4 Below the Radar: Congregations and Volunteering   71
　3.5 Community Assets and Buildings   76

3.6 Evidence from Home and Afield   77
    3.6.1 A New Anglican Philanthropy?   77
    3.6.2 Learning from across the Anglican Communion   78
      - Anglicare Australia   79
      - Brotherhood of St Laurence   81
      - Hong Kong Sheng Kung Hui Welfare Council   82
      - Mainland European and Ecumenical Potential   83

Part Four: Morals, Management, and Commissioning   85
    4.1 Price, Performance and Unconditional Solidarity   85
    4.2 Towards a New 'Prophetic' Challenge?   87
    4.3 Christian Principles for Commissioning   88
      - Sacrifice and Gift   88
      - Covenant and Consistency   89
      - Voice and Prophecy   90
      - Subsidiarity and Empowerment   90
    4.4 The Civic Value Matrix   91

Part Five: Conclusion and Recommendations   95
    5.1 Recommendations   95
      5.1.1 To Number 10   96
      5.1.2 To the Cabinet Office   96
      5.1.3 To the Charity Commission   97
      5.1.4 To the Foreign Office and DfID   97
      5.1.5 To the Archbishops of Canterbury and York   98
      5.1.6 To the Lords Spiritual   98
      5.1.7 To the House of Bishops and the General Synod   98
      5.1.8 To Theological Colleges/Ministerial Training Programmes 99
    5.2 Final Remarks   100

Appendices   103
    A: Faithworks Charter   103
    B: Interim Briefing to Parmjit Dhanda MP   105
    C: Round the Cabinet   109
    D: Regional Studies   119
    E: Timeline of Faith-Founded or Church-Incubated
      Organisations/Projects   131
    F: Dissemination   135

Foreword

It was a government minister and the now Chair of the Conservative party that really convinced me that this piece of work needed doing. Jim Murphy (then a minister at Work and Pensions) suggested to me that the Church of England should take on some responsibility for providing Jobcentre Plus. Then, a few weeks later, Caroline Spelman suggested that as a practising Anglican she would love to see the Church providing services for elderly people suffering from dementia. 'People would have confidence if it was the church looking after granny'. Could we even contemplate moving into this sort of provision? Was there either the ability or the capacity? Would it all be a distraction from mission and evangelism? Would it compromise our prophetic relationship with government and national and local levels? Were government contracting policies appropriate for a relationship with the Church of England?

I was also aware that as always social enterprise was alive and kicking within the dioceses. As I travelled I heard of and saw numerous welfare initiatives, some with contracts or service level agreements, others showing the entrepreneurial skill that the church has displayed over the centuries when faced with poverty, sickness and social and educational deprivation. I also heard that the then Secretary of State for Work and Pensions, John Hutton, had travelled to Australia to look at some of the work undertaken by organisations such as Anglicare, Benetas and the Brotherhood of St Laurence. I also learnt that the Anglican Church in Hong Kong was a major provider of welfare services in partnership with a Communist government.

So this research was born. We had little information about our own capacity as a Church or indeed the level of existing activity. We had only a sketchy idea of political aspirations for our involvement. We needed an informed and reflective assessment of the position for the Church to consider the nature and extent of its future participation. The House of Bishops and its Urban Bishops' Panel, the Mission and Public Affairs Council and the Archbishops' Council were all consulted and lent their support to this work being undertaken. Money was raised and the research commissioned.

I am delighted with the outcome. By any measure it has been a complex and multi-layered process. I was able to make some contribution to it with the help of the Archbishops by looking at the work in Hong Kong and Australia. But for the researchers it became a labour of love, involving them in a much longer and deeper journey than they ever expected. For that I am profoundly grateful because I believe this to be one of the most important reports produced by the Church since *Faith in the City*. It will require study at all levels of the Church and then decision. But it will also need careful political study by all political parties. The Church of England is still a major player in social and welfare provision in this country despite what its detractors might believe. It has earned the right as the largest voluntary organisation (and so much more) in the country to be listened to and worked with as a respected partner in the area of welfare provision as it is in education. For, as the report shows, without it this country would be infinitely poorer.

Stephen Lowe
Bishop of Hulme and Bishop for Urban Life and Faith

Acknowledgements

We acknowledge, firstly, the very generous help we have received throughout this process from Rt Rev Stephen Lowe, Bishop of Hulme and Bishop for Urban Life and Faith. Bishop Stephen not only conceived the idea of this report and commissioned us to undertake it, but regularly made time to meet with us in order to be updated on our progress, share with us the fruits of his own research and meetings, and enable us to reflect with him on our findings. Bishop Stephen visited Australia and Hong Kong in the summer of 2007 to observe the role of the Anglican Church in providing welfare services in those countries and brought back valuable material for our project.

This research would not have been possible without funding, and we thank the Esmée Fairbairn Foundation, the Social Responsibility Division of the Anglican Diocese of Southwark, the Church Community Fund and Sr Anne Thompson and the Daughters of Jesus for their very generous support. We also thank CCLA for hosting a dinner for chief executives that was kindly organised by Stephen Bubb of ACEVO. Barclays Bank hosted a seminar for Ascend at which we tested some of our findings, while students on the Cambridge Masters in Social Enterprise – a group of mid career professionals that includes academics and policy makers, entrepreneurs and third sector activists from Asia, Africa, South America, the West Indies and the EU– also debated and helped shape our draft findings.

Our colleague at the Von Hügel Institute, Dr Jolanta Stankeviciute, contributed enormously to this project by processing survey data, editing the text and offering advice. Terry Drummond CA also gave generous support throughout, making available resources to which we would not otherwise have had access, facilitating funding for the Bishop's commission and sharing his insights with us. We also acknowledge the help of staff at Church House including Mr William Fittall, Revd Dr Malcolm Brown, Revd Dr Andrew Davey, Rev Christopher Jones and Ms Alison Cundiff. Rev Lynda Barley and Rebecca Payne also deserve special mention as does the Stewardship Department. In the field of charity law we have been greatly helped by Stone King LLP, especially Alexandra Whittaker and Robert Mearns, as well as informal conversations with Elizabeth Davis of Blake Lapthorn Tarlo Lyons.

We thank all who shared insights with us at the bishops' residential in Derbyshire including the Archbishop of Canterbury and the bishops of Liverpool, Worcester, and Birmingham. Thanks to those who attended seminars at The Manchester Centre for Public Theology, the Urban Bishops' meeting, the Von Hügel Institute and in London. Not least among our active attendees were the bishops of Oxford, Buckingham, Willesden, Huntington (now Gloucester), Worcester, Leeds, Burnley and Southampton, Lisa Harker (co-Director of the Institute for Public Policy Research), Frank Field MP, Niall Cooper (Director, Church Action on Poverty) and Mgr John Devine (Archdiocese of Liverpool).

We also thank the bishops who replied so fully to our questionnaire exploring their 'civic contribution', and the diocesan chief executives and social responsibility officers who responded to our questions about their 'capacity' and 'experience'.

A large number of people agreed to be interviewed by us in person, by telephone or via e-mail, or helped in some other way, and we thank each for their time and interest: Jan Ainsworth; Lord (David) Alton; Revd Dr Chris Baker (William Temple Foundation); Mr Simon Barrow (Ekklesia); Rt Hon John Battle MP; Revd Chris Beales; Fran Beckett OBE (Church Urban Fund); Professor John Benington (Warwick); Nick Bent; Jonathan Bland (Social Enterprise Coalition); Dr Dan Boucher (CARE); Mr Gary Bradshaw-Mays; Dr Luke Bretherton (King's College London); Beth Breeze; Professor David Bridges (Cambridge); Mr Stephen Bubb (ACEVO); Sam Burke; Alistair Burt MP; Revd Steve Chalke MBE (Faithworks); Angela Cheyne (Age Concern); Greg Clark MP; Mr Niall Cooper (Church Action on Poverty); Mr Graham Dale; Dr Adam Dinham (Anglia Ruskin); David Drew MP; Mark Edney OP; Prof Richard Farnell (University of Coventry); Rt Hon Frank Field MP; Lynda Fisher (Grooms Shaftesbury); Michael Jabez Foster MP; Matthew Frost (TearFund); Ms Alison Gelder (Housing Justice); Prof Elaine Graham (Manchester University); Bill Hampson DL; Sharon Hodgson MP; Veronique Jochum (NCVO); Neil Jameson (Citizens Organising Foundation); Mr Robert Keen; Rev John Kennedy; Ms Pauline Kennedy (Children's Society); Nigel Kettley (NPC); Robert Key MP; Humaiun Kobir (Muslim Council of GB); David Lammy MP; Andrew Lansley CBE, MP; Ms Nola Leech (CARE); Jane Leek; Mr Tim Livesey (Lambeth Palace); Sarah McCarthy-Fry MP; Ms Liz Mariner (PECAN); Lord (Andrew) Mawson; Ms Joy Madeiros (Faithworks); Stephen Matthews (YMCA); Rt Hon Alun Michael MP; Rev Mr Stephen Morgan (RC Diocese of Portsmouth); Mr Alastair Murray (Housing Justice); Dr Bernadette O Keefe; Ms Christine Pattison (Community Action Hampshire); Catherine Pepinster (The Tablet); Lord (Raymond) Plant; Revd Canon Nick Ralph (Diocese of Portsmouth); Andy Reed MP; Canon Chris Rich (Diocese of Guildford); Ms Jo Rice (St Paul's Hammersmith); Mr Paul Richards; Dr Robert Song (Durham); Nick Spencer (Theos); Prof Brian Stanley (Edinburgh); Dr Richard Steenvoorde; Rev Brian Strevens (SCA Health and Care); Rt Hon Stephen Timms MP; Mr Cameron Watt (Centre for Social Justice); Ms Alison

Webster (Diocese of Oxford); Karl Wilding (NCVO); Canon Richard Wheeler; Paul Whitnall (YMCA); Jenny Wingate; Mr Paul Woolley (Theos). We also thank those interviewees from the civil service, Churches and the voluntary sector who requested anonymity.

We would most especially like to thank our families, along with the Principal and community at the Margaret Beaufort Institute of Theology (Cambridge), for their patient support, encouragement and assistance.

A special mention of thanks to Kate Crofts and Pat Gouldstone whose laughter, hard work, and cakes contribute so much to our Institute's success.

During the course of this study, we learned of the passing of two men who in many senses symbolise the strands of service uncovered in this report. Bishop John Austin was a member of the follow-up working parties to the Faith in the City Commission and served on many social justice and statutory bodies in London and the Midlands. His contributions to retreats at Ince Benet were striking both for their ecumenism and their encouragement. Arthur Brookes, an assiduous, kind and loved tutor at St John's College, Durham and a devoted husband/father, volunteered and supported the work of Durham Cathedral. He also stayed active in his Bible study group and continued to find time to write. Both were friends to one of us and both examples to all. We dedicate this report to these two fine Christians and to all those throughout Britain like them.

Centre for the Study of Faith in Society
Von Hügel Institute
College of St Edmund of Abingdon
Cambridge CB3 OBN   *Pentecost Sunday 2008*
www.vhi.org.uk

About the Authors

Francis Davis is co-Director of the Centre for the Study of Faith in Society at the Von Hügel Institute, St Edmund's College, Cambridge. A graduate of Durham, London (SOAS) and Southampton, he is currently a Visiting Fellow in the Centre for Civil Society at the LSE. He was previously founder board member and Chair of a leading social enterprise in the health and social care sector and is on the board of judges for the Erste Stiftung Prize for Social Cohesion in SE Europe. He lectures on the Cambridge Judge Business School/Continuing Education Masters programme in social enterprise and community development and has published on migration, EU social inclusion policies and governance in religious organisations.

Elizabeth Paulhus is a researcher at the Von Hügel Institute, St Edmund's College, Cambridge, and a scholar of the International Young Leaders Network (www.iyln.com). A former Fulbright Scholar in Germany, she graduated *summa cum laude* from Boston College (USA) with a degree in theology. In Autumn 2008 she will begin graduate studies in social policy at the Heller School at Brandeis University, Massachusetts. Her research has focused on churches, social welfare, and issues of migration and justice.

Andrew Bradstock is co-Director of the Centre for the Study of Faith in Society at the Von Hügel Institute, St Edmund's College, Cambridge, and from 2000-2005 was National Secretary for Church and Society for the United Reformed Church. He holds degrees in Theology, Politics and Church History from the Universities of Bristol and Otago and a PhD in Political Theory from the University of Kent at Canterbury. He has lectured in Theology at colleges of higher education in Southampton and Winchester and written and edited a number of books on the relationship between faith and politics.

The Centre for the Study of Faith in Society at the Von Hügel Institute is part academic research centre and part think tank located at St Edmund's College, Cambridge. Its particular strengths are in religion and public policy, religion and conflict resolution, the Churches and migration, education, poverty and social inclusion. Recent activities have included a major international inter-faith colloqium on faith-based education in liberal societies (funded by the Templeton Foundation), a conference on Christian approaches to European security and migration, and lectures by Professor Mary Jo Bane (Harvard), Cardinal Peter Turkson (Ghana) and Dr Mohammed Abdul Bari (Muslim Council of Great Britain).

Introduction

This report was commissioned by the Bishop for Urban Life and Faith, Rt Rev Stephen Lowe, with the full support of the Archbishops' Council of the Church of England, and with the approval of the House of Bishops.

This *exploratory* study aims to enquire into the Church of England's current social contribution and to assess the potential for its involvement in welfare reform, voluntary activity and public service delivery in pursuit of the common good. It goes to the heart of debates about the future direction and identity of our nation and the nature of civic health and vitality. Our interim finding from this study, the first part of a three-phase enquiry, is that when it comes to faith communities in general, and aspects of charity law and social policy in particular, the government is planning blind and failing parts of civil society. This failure, in the view of our respondents, is compounded by key features of the government's current commissioning regime. The government has good intentions, but is moral without a compass.[1]

Preparing this report has involved consulting and interviewing nearly three quarters of the bishops and dioceses in England and more than 250 parliamentarians, civil servants, community activists, chief executives of charities, national umbrella bodies, clergy and academics. The research process has taken us to Manchester, Oxford, London, Southampton, Leeds and Brussels and other locations to conduct seminars and interviews, and we have also carried out new empirical studies and gathered published and unpublished data.

The report will be distributed to every member of General Synod and will be the subject of a national and international programme of dissemination.[2] Several special editions of journals will follow, as well as further studies focused on key questions raised here. Although exploratory in nature, this study is one of the more wide-ranging enquiries into UK Church-Government relations and social welfare in recent years. As such it is an important contribution to wider debates about English identity.

---

1 Gordon Brown's candidacy speech to be leader of the Labour Party, 2007 (excerpt follows): 'I am a conviction politician. Call it "the driving power of social conscience", call it "the better angels of our nature", call it "our moral sense", call it a belief in "civic duty". I joined this party as a teenager because I believed in these values. They guide my work, they are *my moral compass*. This is who I am'. This was intended as a 'mission statement' for the post-Blair era of UK politics.

2 See Appendix F.

PART 1: METHODOLOGY

1.1 Our Brief: A Report for Church and Nation

Our original brief was to prepare a report for the Church of England that could assist its own reflection and contribute to its conversations with Government. The Church – and its critics, such as the National Secular Society - believed that it was being encouraged, at both the national and local level, to become engaged in 'welfare delivery' and to join what some of its members called 'the contract culture'. According to some representatives of the Church it was being enticed into 'doing the state's job'. The Church sensed that major policy changes were afoot and was keen to grasp fully their significance – not least as many of these changes appeared to have a 'faith-based' dimension.

While the Church wanted to understand the policy environment, it also had questions of ecclesiastical principle, theology, governance and resources. Even if it wanted to engage in 'welfare provision' or advocacy, did it have the *capacity* and *ought* it to do so?

A Note On Theology

We consider all of the issues touched upon in this report to have significant theological interest, importance and potential impact. We have spent a good deal of time reflecting upon the work of pioneers in research at the interface of religious life and voluntary action.[3]

However, within the time and resources available in the first phase of our work, it has not been possible to develop a full theological exposition of all of the questions at stake. To have done so without addressing the immense weaknesses in evidence surrounding aspects of the Church would have left sustained theological reflection unrooted in the social and political reality that we were encountering. This is not to

---

3   Malcolm Torry, Helen Cameron and Margaret Harris, for example, pioneered the study of faith-based organisations at the then LSE Centre for Voluntary Organisation until circa 1998 and then developed this work at Aston Business School. See M. Harris & M. Torry (eds) (2000) *Managing Religious and Faith Based Organisations: A Guide To The Literature,* Aston. See also M.J. Bane & B. Coffin (2005) *Taking Faith Seriously* (Harvard); J. Beckford & S. Gilliat, (1998) *Religion in Prison: Equal Rites in a Multi-Faith Society* Cambridge University Press; L. Bretherton (2006) *A New Establishment? Theological Politics and the Emerging Shape of Church-State Relations* Political Theology 7:3; M. Brown & P. Ballard *(eds) (2006) The Church and Economic Life: A Documentary Study* SCM; G. Davie *(1994) Religion in Britain since 1945: Believing without Belonging,* Oxford: Blackwell; R. Plant (2001) *Politics, Theology and History* Cambridge University Press. We also acknowledge the important work of the William Temple Foundation, led by Chris Baker, on 'spiritual capital'. www.wtf.org

say that we have left theological challenges untouched; rather it is simply to note that deeper theological explorations will be featured in subsequent phases of our work.

1.2 The Research Questions

We were asked to ascertain if the government was seeking to encourage the Church of England to engage afresh in 'the contract culture'. We were also asked to consider how the Church might respond to any such approach in 'prophetic political word' and 'practical social action'.[4]

In pursuing answers to these questions we reflected upon aspects of the nature of modern policy making and the challenges it might present for the Church at national, regional and local level. What is the government's policy with respect to the Church, faith communities, and welfare reform? Does the government have an evidence base upon which to build its interaction with faith communities, particularly the Church of England? Should the Church engage in civic contribution, and how should this happen? Does the Church have reliable data about itself (e.g. knowledge of available skills or good practice examples) that it could share with government or other social partners? Finally, does the Church have the capacity to engage, and in what manner, regardless of its inclination?

At the outset we encountered profound mismatches and misperceptions between how the Church understood its current significance, role and potential and the extent to which this was recognised in the policy community. We will outline some of these misperceptions later in the report.

Perhaps even more significantly, we uncovered huge gaps in government evidence about faith communities in general and the churches in particular. We encountered on the part of Government a significant lack of understanding of, or interest in, the Church of England's current or potential contribution in the public sphere. Indeed we were told that Government had consciously decided to focus its evidence gathering almost exclusively on minority religions. We were unsurprised to hear that some of these consequently felt 'victimised'.[5]

We also found the Charity Commission's data and systems of classification to be very weak, while again a conscious focus on minority communities was being achieved to

---

4   We have drawn throughout on F. Davis (2004cohort) *Can A Church Create Public Value?* (Warwick IGPM). This paper is unpublished.

5   Interview. Henceforth, where the reference 'interview' appears without a name, it refers to an interviewee who requested anonymity.

the relative exclusion of the Christian church and hundreds of other charities. Three separate government departments admitted to possessing 'no evidence base' on the Christian churches, despite one having proactively commissioned new research to underpin its faith-based agenda.[6] The Office of the Third Sector could not conceive why such an evidence base might be necessary, despite ministerial claims of taking faith communities seriously.

Given the extent to which modern departments of state aspire to root their strategies in sound research and hard data[7] it is unsurprising that these omissions are now beginning to contribute to weaknesses in public policy design and coordination.

In view of this finding we devoted an increased amount of time to drawing together some initial evidence that those active in debates relating to faith-based policy reform appear to lack and which the Church would need if it was to speak with meaningful clarity to the broader policy and third sector communities. This involved a close analysis of aspects of the government's policy priorities and the gathering of data resources scattered across the Church itself, which themselves had been caught in departmental 'silos'. These are set out later in our argument.

For these reasons, the report reaches beyond the Church to government at national and local levels, as well as to umbrella bodies in the voluntary sector. It should also be of interest to observers and students of the voluntary sector, faith communities and public governance in the 21st century.

1.3 The Research Process and Methods

- First, we made a brief survey of the historical background to current welfare debates and conducted a deeper study of the government's current policy priorities. In both cases this included a literature review, a review of key policy documents, and interviews.

- Second, we used published and unpublished sources to explore the nature and extent of the Anglican institutional presence in England. This was of particular importance in our enquiry as Mission and Public Affairs, our key link department in Church House, was undergoing a leadership interregnum as the study started. As a result, the department could not furnish an up-to-

---

6   J. Beckford et al (2006) *Review of the Evidence Base on Faith Communities* ODPM.

7   H. Davies et al (ed) (2000) *What Works: Evidence Based Policy and Practice in Public Services* Policy Press.

date database of Diocesan social responsibility officers, social projects run by the Church or social enterprises functioning on the ground.[8]

- Third, we held a plenary session with the Anglican Bishops of England, Wales, Scotland and Ireland and led a workshop for 40 of them. We also ran consultative seminars in different regions to debate the key questions of this study and to ascertain views from all sections of the Church.

- Fourth, we sent questionnaires to each diocese in order to ascertain financial resources, experience of contracting and management skills, qualifications and capacities. We asked how far each diocese had progressed in the conversation about reporting their 'public benefit' in future annual returns to the Charity Commission. We also asked about their attitudes to increasing the Church's involvement in the 'commissioning state' agenda.

- Fifth, we examined cathedrals, which in terms of governance stand largely separate from both parishes and dioceses. We utilised websites and other published data to determine the usage and contributions of cathedrals for both Church and civil society activities.[9]

- Sixth, using published data we explored the relative institutional significance of better-known Christian charities in order to compare them with their so-called 'mainstream' counterparts. This involved recording their membership figures as declared on websites, in annual reports and returns to statutory bodies, and in the press.

- Seventh, we wrote to every diocesan and suffragan bishop asking each to state the contribution he had made in recent years to the work of regional and local charities, civil society and to public bodies, both within and beyond the 'Christian community'.

- Lastly, we drew on case studies, examples and individual interviews with policy makers, politicians, voluntary sector leaders, church activists and leaders to gain a clearer picture of the range and form of local and regional action on the part of Anglican bodies.

8   We note that William Fitall has been seeking to move Church House along an evidence-based policy route, not least with research support from Rev Lynda Barley and Rebecca Payne, and we commend these efforts to readers. The National Institute for Christian Education (a network of Church colleges and universities) led by Professor James Arthur at Canterbury Christ Church University College, has made a start in this direction but, in the words of those in Church House, 'needs additional resources' to meet the Church's real research needs.

9   We also undertook a national survey of charity chief executives to determine their motivating principles and values, but despite the time expended, the response rate was too low to merit inclusion in this study.

1.4 Research Factors

1.4.1 Congregations or Institutions?

At the launch of the government's FaithAction initiative in February 2008, Rt Hon Stephen Timms MP, Minister of State for Employment and Welfare Reform, affirmed the social action of religious grassroots bodies, praising them as representatives of a 'new social movement'.[10] FaithAction itself is a loose and low capacity network of congregations, smaller voluntary bodies and freelance consultants which, we were told, was likely to lose key allies the moment the first wave of its funding came to an end.[11] The Department of Communities and Local Government (DCLG) has spoken of the importance of the UK's 54,000 places of worship and of local inter-faith partnerships,[12] while we were told that Prime Minister Gordon Brown believes many religious groups are 'part of a new progressive consensus'.[13] Meanwhile, the Charity Commission launched a full consultation with minority faith communities for a number of reasons, but notably as a consequence of governance work with Muslim and independent evangelical 'congregations'.[14] *Local* religious enthusiasm and action were also interests of the 2007 report of the Commission for Integration and Cohesion.[15]

This focus on 'congregations' by policy makers seemed useful but inadequate to us for several reasons. First, pioneers in the study of UK faith-based organisations have expressed profound reservations concerning the potential of 'congregations' to engage in welfare reform, social cohesion action and public service contracting because of their limited scale and skills or the possibility that these might lead to localised 'faith competition'.[16] The government's focus suggests that it has not adequately learned from research that suggests that state engagement with local congregations can distort their identity and potential civic contribution, causing more harm than good. This remains the case despite the efforts of recent DCLG draft guidance on commissioning and faith organisations.

---

10 From a speech by S. Timms MP (2008) at FaithAction's *'Procurement Ready'* launch conference.

11 Interview with Faithworks. As later comments show Faithworks achieves huge impact despite its relatively small size.

12 DCLG (2007) *Face to Face and Side by Side: A Framework for Interfaith Dialogue and Social Action.*

13 Interview with Cabinet advisor.

14 Charity Commission (2007) *Working With Faith Groups* op cit.

15 Commission for Integration and Cohesion (June 2007) *'Our Shared Future'.*

16 C. Rochester (2006) *Making Sense of Volunteering: A Literature Review* Volunteering England; M. Harris (with P. Halfpenny & C. Rochester) (2003) *An Expanded Role for Faith-Based Organisations? Lessons from the UK Jewish Voluntary Sector.* Journal of Social Policy, 32 (1), pp. 93-112; *Face to Face* op cit.

Second, we were aware that the Church of England is not simply a 'network of individual congregations' like some independent evangelical denominations; rather, it is an institutional body with an episcopal structure in which dioceses are important administrative – and theological – units and cathedrals have great institutional autonomy. It seemed important to us to take this into account.

Third, we were aware of international social science literature that suggested a relationship between a religion's structure as an institution, its theology and the form and sustainability of its political advocacy, pastoral work and other activities.[17] Borer's study of the Churches in South Africa, for example, suggested that while the Council of Churches was able to move quickly to oppose apartheid because of its democratic and national structure, it had to work harder than more centralised and internationalised religions to sustain this position. This self-same structure meant that the adopted position of 'opposition' could be regularly contested and so was harder to hold firm.[18] In the United States, Jim Wallis' view that Christian congregations are an 'organisable constituency' is highly influenced by the denominational structures and insights of his own faith.[19]

We questioned then whether the 'congregational' emphasis of Government (and Opposition) policy would suffice when it came to assessing the role and potential of the Church of England in welfare organisation and other civic contributions. What significant assets did the wider institutional – and theologically significant - structure bring into play for both state and Church? We believed that defining the largest religious institution in England as a collection of 'congregations' was the empirical equivalent of saying that the NHS was simply a collection of GPs' surgeries.

1.4.2 Social Capital and the Omission of Capability

The other key factor that we had to consider was the government's expressed enthusiasm for Robert Putnam's important work on social capital, particularly as outlined in his seminal book, *Bowling Alone: The Collapse and Revival of American Community.*[20]

---

17 For example, T.A. Borer (1998) *The Church Struggle* University of Notre Dame; P. Gifford (1998) *African Christianity: Its Public Role* C Hurst; T. Reese (1992) *A Flock of Shepherds: The National Conference of Catholic Bishops* Rowman and Littlefield.

18 Borer op cit.

19 J. Wallis *What's An FBO?* In E.J. Dionne & J.J. Dilulio (eds) 2000 *What's God Got to Do with the American Experiment?* Brookings Institute.

20 R. Putnam (2000) *Bowling Alone: The Collapse And Revival of American Community* Simon and Schuster.

19

Putnam and his followers typically refer to three types of social capital that are needed to produce the well-connected community:[21]

- Bonding: social ties that link people together with others who are primarily like them along some key dimension.
- Bridging: social ties that link people together with others across a cleavage that typically divides society.
- Linking: a social tie (often a bridging social tie) to those with power that provides one with the capacity to gain access to resources, ideas and information from formal institutions beyond the community.

Ideas of social capital receive active use in some faith quarters[22] and profound criticism in others.[23] Our primary interest was the fact that the government was using this framework to encourage dialogue *between* faith groups to enhance 'social cohesion' without applying a nuanced understanding of the varying attributes these faith groups bring to the table of public discourse. We encountered many stories demonstrating the immense effort and trouble involved in simply bringing religious groups with disproportionate skills, resources and other capacities together to 'bridge'. Such work can overstretch smaller religious entities while simultaneously disempowering larger ones, such as the Church of England. In the long term, we heard, this can lead to a reduction in civic health, especially when 'bridging' is limited to a very small number of individuals in a local congregation.[24]

In our view recent research for the London Borough of Lewisham supports the idea that partnering between faith groups and councils must go beyond just a simplistic view of social capital, which is unrelated to social capability and impact. In 2002, the Local Government Association (LGA) congratulated Lewisham on its approach to working with faith groups: conferences, publications and the setting up of a small fund to support faith organisations' contribution to the wider community (play schemes, gospel choirs, etc) were well received. After initial enthusiasm, however, research found that both council officials and faith leaders felt that the work had 'reached a plateau' and that people had become tired of dialogue and wanted action

---

21 Definitions from online glossary of the Saguaro Seminar, which can be found at: http://www.hks. harvard.edu/saguaro/glossary.htm
22 R. Furbey et al (2006) Faith As Social Capital: Connecting or dividing? Rowntree
23 A. Davey (2007) 'Faithful Cities: Locating Everyday Faithfulness' in Contact, 152, pp.8-20.
24 *Faith as Social Capital* (2006) op cit.

that made a difference.[25] Capability, sustainability, funding and results proved to be of equal importance to ideas of bridging and bonding social capital.

The well-intentioned attempt on the part of Government to encourage cross-community conversation in one policy area did not necessarily lead to assessing the comparative capacities of each religious group to contribute to civic health and wellbeing, nor the principles, form and structures for doing so. It also risked confusing consultation with action and meeting for meeting's sake.[26] We were told that while such capacity studies had been undertaken by Government with regard to British Islam, similar studies had not been carried out for any of the UK's largest faith communities.[27]

This absence of a rich inter-religious institutional mapping, along with a full assessment of contrasting capabilities was, we were told, beginning to restrict Anglican civic contributions. The Church of England was often bracketed alongside bodies that were comparatively much smaller and which could not draw on similar theologies, motivations, skills and capabilities.

Consequently, in looking at the Church's potential as a public agent or social partner, we sought to make an exploratory assessment of its social capabilities. Social capital theory, at least in so far as we encountered its use by Government, needed complementary data and frameworks. The scale of Anglican presence and its structure both within and beyond localities, combined with its open theologies, seemed to place the Church of England in a category of its own, rather than under the simple blanket of 'faith groups' where some had placed it.[28]

1.4.3 The Church's Clash of Self-Perceptions

It became clear to us during the early stages of our research that much debate existed within the leadership of the Church regarding the relative virtues of what some called 'appropriate' public sector change and others the 'inappropriate' 'marketisation of love'.

Echoing the sentiments of some within the Church, one respondent said, 'it is not the Church's job to be useful or to put right government failures. Our job is to be

---

25   R. Farnell (2007) *Faith In Lewisham – A Review and Evaluation of Partnership Work between London Borough of Lewisham and Local Faith groups* Coventry University/Lewisham Borough Council.

26   Farnell op cit.

27   Interview government advisor.

28   A. Dinham (2008) Presentation to East of England Voluntary Organisations, kindly sent to the authors. The work of Dinham, supported by Lord Tyler, is to be commended. http://www.faithsunit. org

prophetic and call for social justice'. Throughout the country we met Anglicans who rejected the idea 'that care can be measured' or given a 'cash value'.

One senior bishop thought the commissioning state was 'a cross-party conspiracy designed to undermine local democracy'. Other bishops passionately expressed the view that 'privatisation is immoral', and one Episcopal advisor wrote in strident terms that, in his view, 'the very idea of looking at Church-state partnership is predicated on a misunderstanding… because our political class are not to be trusted'. The Church and Society Officer in the Diocese of St Albans approached the problem from a different perspective, saying, 'the trouble is that the civil service just have no idea about how tough it can be on the ground and when dealing with local statutory offices… They have just spent so little time on the streets'. This insight arose from years of experience as a priest in the inner city, echoing sentiments expressed by many whom we visited.[29]

Bad local experiences of the Church 'contracting' with the Manpower Services Commission in the 1980s and then being 'left high and dry when the funding ran out' were frequently mentioned, as were references to local government departments treating churches with 'suspicion' and subjecting them to 'discrimination'. For example, we repeatedly heard of local authorities that would not even entertain conversation with local churches regarding social action. One county council equalities officer told us *sotto voce* that, 'churches are just not good for society'.

Others within the Church, however, could not wait to 'embrace the social enterprise agenda more fully'. One bishop said, 'we need to be more entrepreneurial', while a clergyperson commented that 'the Church and the voluntary sector couldn't run some parts of the welfare state as badly as local government if they tried'.

Many within this second camp spoke of thriving, successful programmes that had continued for many years and had been the bedrock of wide-ranging initiatives. Several expressed strong reservations about those who criticised their experiences with the Manpower Services Commission. One interviewee, for example, reflected that 'the trouble' with those who had complained was that:

> Some took resources and thought that life would never change again… while others were both scanning the future and doing creative things. This meant that they could respond when change came… For many who went under

---

29 This Officer had been a key influence in the development of local authority anti-poverty strategies in the wake of *Faith in the City*. Collaborating with Rev John Harrison and then Cllr (now Cabinet Minister) John Denham, this work led to major joint local government/Church projects.

> it was a question of over-trading… or the wrong people trying to do the right thing… poor management or poor judgement or behaving as though a contract with accountability clauses was the same as a grant or a gift.

Still others thought that the scepticism about the policy direction of all parties was a consequence of the Church's lack of specialism in modern public policy problems and challenges. A government advisor, who is also an active member of the Church of England, asserted that:

> the problem is the quality of advice the Church has been getting… In here (civil service)… the quality of training and the skills expected are very high, but then sometimes we are sent a vicar with merely an interest in politics or people without policy track records… It is very hard to have a conversation with those with no relevant experience… the mismatch of experience is terrible.

The National Council for Voluntary Organisations (NCVO) reiterated this problem regretting the Church's lack of a truly modern understanding of policy and Government's direction of travel. 'If the Church is worried about the "contract culture" that would suggest the need for more awareness. It is a phrase that is hardly used now that we are in the era, for good or bad, of Best Value and the Compact'. The Church may need to ensure that its language and understanding are up-to-date. One of the most senior voluntary sector figures in the country boldly said, 'bishops may want to turn the clock back but the world has moved on - they will just have to get real'.

Significantly, even in places where the local bishop was expressing moral reservations about 'contracting', the Church was providing services in some way. We wondered whether this 'low key', 'below the radar' approach was representative of the Church as a whole.

With this lively debate running within the Church, it was surprising that 65% of the dioceses that replied to our questionnaire admitted that they had not yet discussed the clauses in the new Charity Act which require the Church of England, for the first time, to demonstrate formally its 'public benefit'. This new requirement in charity reporting puts traditional debates about the nature of Church in a new context. 'Advancing religion' is now only charitable if its 'public benefit' can be demonstrated by an 'evidence-based approach', and the quality and veracity of such evidence is, according to the Charity Commission, likely to be subject to external scrutiny by independent experts from time to time. This is a major change from the previous legal position where 'the advancement of religion' was 'assumed' to be for the public benefit as of right. These are new times and, at the least, the retention of charity status will require new approaches in reporting.

A former senior civil servant argued that, 'even without public benefit we will never go back to a world of no measurement or accountability… to suggest this as a serious option would be, at the least, naïve… the question is how can we find ways of recording the wonderful things churches can do so that they can be demonstrated more broadly'.

Nevertheless we did encounter certain unanimity in one area of our research. Every participant in our study from the Church agreed that there was deep 'religious illiteracy' on the part of Government, especially on the local level, and that an increased tendency to centralised mega-contracts in some government departments was bad for the whole of the voluntary sector.

1.4.4 Challenges to the Church's Perception

What was also relatively uncontested within the Church was its perception that it is an institution which 'is present in every community in the land', which 'holds the memory of communities' and whose parish clergy 'have a special bond with the places in which they work'. We also frequently heard Church people assert that 'the care offered by Christians is special because, unlike secular efforts, churches care for the whole person' and that 'there is an extra love present that people are aware of and know about'. Even among those who suggested to us that the Church is now on the margins of society – that 'Christendom' is finished or at least dying – ideas of rootedness, an extra 'value added' or a 'special care' were enthusiastically articulated. This 'value added' claim was so frequently claimed – and contested – that we shall return to it in our recommendations and the second phase of our work.

Yet this self-perception was strongly questioned by some who were not linked to the Church. The NCVO told us that, based on their research, the claim on the part of people of faith that they brought 'extra value' to social care and action 'is unproven'. A senior civil servant related how she associated the Church with closed and closing urban buildings rather than people, life and presence. At the Cabinet Office there was a lack of clarity about whom they would consult regarding the Christian Churches other than the CEO of the Church Urban Fund or a senior figure at Faithworks. One Christian Labour MP even found it revelatory that the Church could actually be engaged in public service reform.

It seemed that Government and the Church have two dissonant understandings of faith. On the one hand, strands within Government view religion as an 'idea' in a marketplace of competing 'values', something associated with a particular building and a particular day of the week. On the other, many Christians attempt to work out principles of faith through institutions, communities, and organisations in every neighbourhood and 'place' throughout the week. The Archdeacon of Leicester is an example of the latter strand. As chair of the New Deal project in former Cabinet minister Patricia Hewitt's seat, he led a major turnaround of the local New Deal programme - an achievement that reportedly even featured in cabinet conversations. 'I did this because I am a priest', he said, 'but I expect that many people think I left the Church behind on Sunday… which is ironic because the Bishop of Leicester suggested I take it on because of our shared belief that *a crisis for the New Deal and the City was a crisis for the Church of the place too.*'

A primary focus in this exploratory study is to take seriously the latter self-articulation of religiosity. We consequently record key examples of the extent of the Church's current contributions in civil society. Although it was not our task to delineate a sociology of 'religious belief', we believe that the evidence we have gathered firmly challenges the conception – often present in our political and civil service interviews - of observant 'faith' as a private orientation without public consequences or civic benefits.

In passing, it is notable that in the 2001 census, 80% of the country said that they believed in God,[30] while an average of 71.8% said they believed in the *Christian* God. According to the National Secular Society,[31] this figure has been overstated by about 20%. Such a claim, given without explanation, fails to take into account the significant regional variations in belief revealed in Figure 1. In the eyes of the media God may be 'dead', but overall in England (not least in Labour strongholds) it would seem that Christianity still is acknowledged as having a role to play in individual value systems.

---

30 S. Timms (2008) op cit.

31 On the NSS website: 'We believe this (religious influence in Government) puts the large minority (*maybe even a majority*) of the population who are not religious at a disadvantage and at risk of having religion forced on them'. Downloaded May 8th 2008.

Figure 1: Percentage of people in England who are Christian, by parish

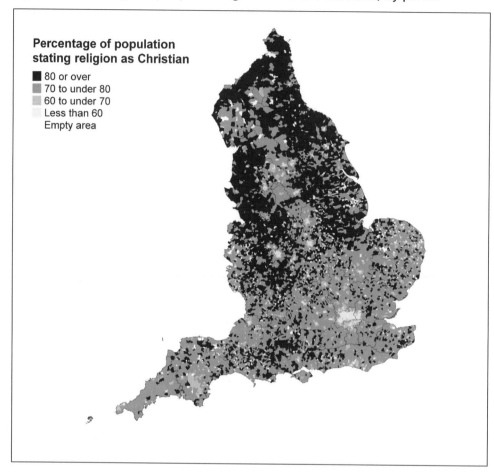

Data source: 2001 Key Statistics. Census Output is reproduced with the permission of the Controller of HMSO and the Queen's Printer for Scotland.

1.4.5 Social Voices and Representation

We note later that according to the Home Office, there is a positive correlation between religious observance and a willingness to volunteer.[32] In subsequent sections we describe a number of institutional factors in Anglican life. In this section, we turn briefly to compare the size and scope of several Christian organisations with their secular counterparts.

32 Citizenship Survey 2005.

26

The following chart maps the membership and total income of just a few examples within a certain income range (up to £250,000,000). Faith-based organisations are marked with an asterisk, and are among the most significant in terms of membership, income or both. This chart also does not reflect the reported £500,000 unrestricted annual revenues of Anglican parishes, nor their nearly one million active members. In the case of Faithworks, we have not included the turnover of their Academies or planned Academies, which add significant revenues and 'customers' to the listed assets.

Interestingly, among the least significant organisations are a number of secular lobby groups whose public profiles are out of proportion to their income, assets or membership base. Please note, since the National Secular Society does not publish its financials, an estimate was determined by multiplying the membership by the annual fees, then adding the donations and bequests reported on the NSS website. The Conservative Party is not listed as we have been unable to ascertain its membership numbers.

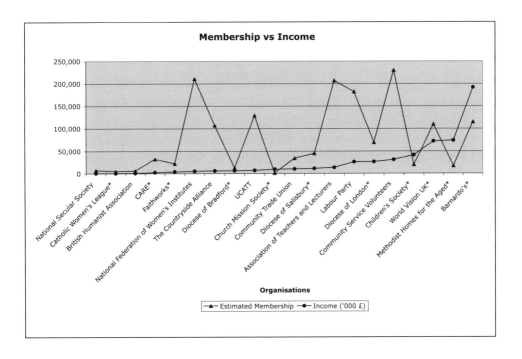

PART 2: FROM PAST TO PRESENT: THE DEVELOPMENT OF MODERN WELFARE ORGANISATION

2.1 The Historical Context

History is crucial for Christian theology. In this section we turn to the way that the Christian community and the government have addressed questions of welfare and action as a means of putting present debates in context.

For many years the issue of how social welfare in Britain should be organised has been highly contested. What balance should be struck between 'individual responsibility' and 'community' or 'collective' provision? What should be the respective roles of central, local and parish government, of charitable resources, of mutuality, of firms and enterprises and – not least – of the Church?

With Britain's integration into the global economy, this terrain remains no less contested, not least as the so-called 'post-war welfare consensus' has been shattered, and the public, private and voluntary sectors now seek to tease out the appropriate means by which to secure welfare and justice in new times in order to protect the vulnerable against today's social risks and challenges.

From the earliest times the Church has organised activities we now group under the generic term 'welfare'. Until the twentieth century it was the main provider in areas like education, health and poverty relief through its schools, hospitals and almshouses. Institutions established by the Church and religious orders as long ago as the Middle Ages continue today to offer the services they were initially set up to provide.

The idea that the state might assume responsibility for aspects of human welfare emerged most strongly in the latter years of the nineteenth century. The Church's incapacity to meet a rapidly increasing demand for schools, together with a concern about living conditions in towns and rural areas, led to the introduction of state education and legislation like the Housing of the Working Classes Act of 1890. The process developed apace during the Liberal administrations of H.H. Asquith and Lloyd George, with measures to introduce pensions (1908) and unemployment insurance (1911).

The post-Second World War welfare state was therefore not a new creation, though it did mark the triumph of the more 'statist' strand in attempts at welfare. For the first time a whole raft of services, covering education, health, income support, personal social services and housing, were to be funded by taxation and 'scientifically administered' by central and local government. While William Beveridge envisaged the continuing private provision of some welfare services, urged the state to encourage voluntary action and favoured a mutual insurance principle in welfare design, Clement Attlee's government set about a wholesale nationalisation of certain services and the extension of state action and ownership into other areas.[33]

The Welfare State was a creature of its time, the era of post-war reconstruction. There was a sense in 1945 that, having fought together to win the War, the nation now needed to work together to win the peace. The particular demands of the War had led to a hitherto unprecedented level of government intervention and control over people's lives, and this arguably eased the way for the State to adopt a comparable level of oversight once it was over. Shared experience of the economic hardship of the interwar years, and the fear and anxiety it generated, also suggested that affording citizens protection from the worst consequences of economic instability should be a government priority. Thus the welfare state of the 1940s and 1950s enjoyed wide popular support and legitimacy. The need to guarantee the basics of life – food, clothing, power – was high on the agenda of most families, who demonstrated a readiness to accept welfare provision as offered by the state, including council housing and a basic pension.

Parts of the Church of England played a major role in creating the final form in which the welfare state emerged. Through the Malvern Conference of 1941, the Archbishop's conference of industrial and economic experts, and, most notably, through his best-selling book *Christianity and Social Order*, Archbishop William Temple was an important advocate for the foundations of the post-war consensus and the Keynesian bureaucratic state.[34]

It was Temple who coined the expression 'welfare state' in contradistinction to the 'power state'. For Temple it was a fundamental duty of government to ensure that all families were adequately housed, that all children had equal access to education and that everybody enjoyed sufficient income to maintain reasonable living conditions. These goals, Temple argued, could be met through high rates of taxation on unearned income together with the nationalisation of the banking system.

Such a system implied central planning but some questions remained. How was the planning authority to be constituted? And through what channels was it to operate?

---

33 J. Harris (1977) *William Beveridge: A Biography*, Oxford (Clarendon).
34 W. Temple (1942) *Christianity and Social Order*, Penguin.

Indeed, it has been suggested that a core feature of this new 'Keynesian welfare state consensus' was its conviction that the civil service would be 'expert' and 'neutral' and that its hierarchically organised and specialist functions would rationally administer the raising of taxes on the one hand and their distribution to increase the sum of human justice on the other.

It is possible to exaggerate the extent to which the welfare settlement under Attlee enjoyed a wide consensus and thus that the 'Anglican mood' on welfare was a national one, both in the Church or wider society. While the aspiration to a form of collective action through state policies clearly prevailed in the immediate post-War years - and was still to be found informing the thinking of 'one nation' Conservatives like Butler and Macmillan and moderate Labour figures like Gaitskell ten years later – the consensus did not lack its critics. For example, in 1944 Friedrich von Hayek published his seminal *The Road to Serfdom,* comprising one of the most compelling neo-liberal critiques of the growing government apparatus of the time, which he saw as a threat to 'freedom'.[35] During the same time period, the author of the 1945 Labour manifesto, Michael Young, retreated to the East End to create what is today the Young Foundation, complaining of an obsession with 'big-ism' in government driven at the expense of more local mutual endeavour.[36]

While critics of bureaucracy and an overweening state on the right and the moderate left were not scarce, aspects of their arguments were given particular momentum by some studies which suggested that the state was actually replicating some of the inequalities that it was intended to overcome. For example, progressive and thoughtful analyses of the politics of mass council housing provision suggested that so called 'welfare state' policies were being driven as much by an unholy alliance of large architects and builders, professional associations, expansive political rhetoric and bureaucratic overload as by any genuine response to need. Moreover, systems of allocation under the welfare state were as likely to generate inequalities as the injustices they were supposed to correct.[37] The New Left activists of the early 1970s community development projects took these complaints further, objecting to a full blown 'capture' of 'the capitalist state' by elite social forces, while advocates of

35 F. Hayek (1944) *The Road to Serfdom,* Routledge.

36 P. Wilmott *Resolving the Dilemma of Bigness* (2005) in G. Dench, T. Flower and K. Gavron (eds) *Young At Eighty - The Prolific Life of Michael Young,* Carcanet.

37 P. Dunleavy (1981) *The Politics of Mass Housing in Britain: Study of Corporate Power and Professional Influence in The Welfare State,* Oxford Clarendon.

'public choice' suggested an equivalent likelihood of failure because of the 'rents' likely to be extracted from welfare states[38] by rapacious civil society forces.

At the same time Christian social innovators and radicals were prominent in pointing to state and market failures and calling for new legislation and models of working via a fresh wave of caring, advocacy, fundraising and social enterprise bodies. The Rev Chad Varah founded the Samaritans. Frank Field led the new Child Poverty Action Group and then the Low Pay Unit from 1969 until 1980. Fr Ken Leech established Centrepoint, while Fr Eamonn Casey was key to the creation of Shelter. The National Cyrenians grew from the work of the Simon Community, while in the overseas development field CAFOD, Christian Aid, SCIAF and Tearfund were founded in 1962, 1964, 1965 and 1968 respectively.[39] By 1974 Tearfund had provided the start-up funds for Tearcraft, from which Richard Adams subsequently built Traidcraft 'to express the principles of love and justice fundamental to the Christian faith'. Today Traidcraft plc is one of the nation's most pioneering social enterprises. In 1977 Church-based housing organisations were key instigators in ensuring the passage of the Homeless Persons Act, the first legislation to provide rights to shelter for the homeless.[40]

Societal changes and the aforementioned struggles of delegitimation of the state began to render centrally funded and administered welfare provision politically indefensible and economically unviable. Will Hutton observed that, 'without either constitutional protection or the commitment of the political class, the welfare state would be vulnerable once the political circumstances of its creation had passed away'.[41] But it was only after the 1974 OPEC oil crisis and the appeal by Labour Chancellor Denis Healey for financial aid from the International Monetary Fund that momentum really began to build for a fundamental realignment of the old consensus. Building on the Labour government's cuts in public spending, the networks of what became known as the 'New Right' took significant steps to capture the moral high ground of political debate and policy through seminars, think tanks and astounding intellectual entrepreneurship. Arthur Seldon and Sir Keith Joseph made striking contributions and found in Margaret Thatcher (and Ronald Reagan in the US) their champions of a new policy direction and of a new morality of 'neo-liberalism'.[42]

---

38 P. Dunleavy and B O Leary (1987) *Theories of the Welfare State- The Politics of Liberal Democracy* McMillan; R. Mishra (1984) *The Welfare State In Crisis* Harvester.

39 In some cases these bodies had predecessors, but these dates indicate when they assumed their modern form.

40 Housing Justice.

41 W. Hutton (1995) '*The State We're In*', p.49, Vintage.

42 D. Marquand (1988) *The Unprincipled Society* Fontana; R. Plant & K. Hoover (1989) *Conservative*

The challenge for the Church in the 1980s was to accept that the welfare state needed radical transformation now that the political (and economic) circumstances of its creation had passed. It is not at all clear that the Church did accept this, taking as evidence the report of the Archbishop's Commission on Urban Priority Areas, *Faith in the City*,[43] published in 1985, and the Board of Social Responsibility's enquiry the following year, *Not Just for the Poor: Christian Perspectives on the Welfare State.*[44] While the latter – as its title suggests - clearly endorsed the concept of welfare for all and accepted a 'mixed economy' of welfare provision, it saw as 'essential' a 'firm framework of public welfare services' and the 'generous provision of services by society through the state'. In a similar vein, the authors of *Faith in the City* refused to countenance cuts in state expenditure and expressed a clear belief in a close correlation between the amount of taxation a state raised and the public good it engendered. Inherent in the political economy of *Faith in the City* is an attachment to the traditional neutral and social democratic Keynesian welfarism for which Archbishop Temple had fought so hard. A small lobby group took up the cause with its later campaign entitled 'Hearing the Cry of the Poor' which lamented the rise in social and income inequality in UK society.

Some voices within the Church, though, sensed that its responses were somehow missing the mark. The old wineskins of post-war theology were being split apart by the force of new developments in thought and policy, and the Church was simply hiding its head in the sand by not recognising them. This included a number of Conservatives who wanted actively to defend the authenticity and morality of their position and to help modernise the Church's views while holding on to what they understood to be key principles from the past.[45] It also included Anglicans who had a strong social vision but thought that many of the Church's 'radicals' were in fact speaking to an agenda that was in tatters and to a world that had moved on.

Among the most profound of the latter was a group established by the Diocese of Winchester, involving Raymond (later Lord) Plant, who published their work formally in a book edited by Canon Anthony Harvey.[46] Plant would go on to argue

---

Capitalism in Britain and the US: A Critical Appraisal Routledge.

43 Archbishop of Canterbury's Commission on Urban Priority Areas (1985) Faith in the City: A Call for Action by Church and Nation, Church House Publishing.

44 Social Policy Committee of the Board of Social Responsibility (1986) Not Just for the Poor: Christian Perspectives on the Welfare State, Church House Publishing.

45 M. Alison & D. Edwards (eds) (1990) *Christianity and Conservatism: Are Christianity and Conservatism Compatible?* London, Hodder & Stoughton; R. Harris (1989) *The Conservative Community: The Roots of Thatcherism - and its Future,* Centre for Policy Studies.

46 A. Harvey (ed) (1989) *Theology in the City,* London, SPCK.

that for those with a commitment to social justice it was no longer adequate simply to state that inequality was 'wrong'. In New Right thinking, he suggested, autonomous individuals make individual and incommensurable choices in the market place, the consequences of which are unintended and thus *morally neutral*. To impose some 'socially just outcome' on this infinite variety of actions would be to assert a collective morality where neo–liberals believed none existed. This would therefore impede individuals from being 'free' to choose what constituted the good life and a good decision. Since there are in a market an immeasurable number of views as to what virtue may consist of, such an imposition would, in the New Right view, itself be an immoral act against liberty.[47]

In partially acknowledging the New Right argument, Plant recognised its implications for the traditional defence of a welfare state that had striven – at least rhetorically - to establish 'equality of outcome'. If the means by which to articulate a common morality – a consensus – were broken or had never existed, then the basis upon which to ground traditional policy actions of a 'collective' nature was no longer present. Arguing from within the progressive tradition Plant consequently advocated 'equality of opportunity' as the fullest conception of justice that can be defended in these new times. One can see New Labour's fascination with 'education' being the crucial platform for lifetime security as one policy consequence of this nuanced progressive perspective.

Arguably in the late eighties and early nineties, those who professed strong 'radical social concerns' in the Church came to epitomise what Giddens characterised as the 'new conservatives'.[48] While they may have lamented the Church's 'lack of understanding of economics',[49] it seemed that what they really regretted was the wider abandonment of Keynesianism. As 'revolutionary' neo-liberalism swept the planet, traditional social democrats and socialists sought to 'conserve' the welfarism with which they had been reared. Whether they expressed this through the traditional language of social responsibility, out of a sense of urban pastoral concern or via an anglicised liberation theology, it seemed they were fighting a losing battle.

It is unclear how unified and numerous these 'new conservatives' were. While Bishop David Sheppard and others gained national prominence and national followings in their defence of the urban poor, radical networks such as the Industrial Mission

---

47 R. Plant (1989) *Socialism, Markets and End States* in S. Estrin and J. Le Grand (eds) *Market Socialism* Oxford (Clarendon).

48 A. Giddens (1994) *Beyond Left And Right - The Future of Radical Politics* Polity.

49 M. Brown & P. Ballard op cit.

Movement peaked with only 122 clergy out of a national total almost 100 times that figure.[50]

But even as the Church of England continued to defend the neutral welfare state with its 'rational' allocative structures that *claimed* to raise taxes in direct proportion to the amount of justice it could deliver, and even as Raymond Plant and colleagues sought to explain that such an approach no longer spoke to the social reality, two complementary strands of development were taking place. Michael Heseltine at the Department for the Environment, in collaboration with ministers Robert Key and Alistair Burt, both Christians, worked not only to reorient the level of state expenditure on welfare, but also to introduce new measurement strategies to ensure 'efficient delivery' and legitimacy in public bureaucracy.[51] The 'new public management' had arrived. While some in the Churches would call this 'more marketisation', it developed complementary strands that merited (and continue to merit) a more nuanced analysis by any Christian with even a basic theological interest in stewardship.

Under John Major's premiership, initiatives such as the chartermark and enhanced public service quality standards could not be categorised as 'left' or 'right'. Indeed, as what became the New Labour project took root a new consensus began to emerge that a fresh approach to markets and a new approach to government were needed as new risks and economic patterns now dominated the social reality.[52]

Across Europe models of welfare provision had come under pressure by major changes in the social and demographic structure of European society: a feminisation of the workforce, a leap in the number of part-time and insecure jobs, and a move away from hierarchically organised manufacturing production. The rise of 'new family forms' due to increased divorce, decreased birth rates and single parent households was creating new patterns of need. In addition an increase in the number of older people raised questions about the sustainability of 'welfare states' and pension funds that rely on inter-generational transfers of taxation and the maintenance of European output.[53] Unsurprisingly this meant similar movements to enhance 'government

---

50 D. Sheppard (2003) *Steps Along Hope Street: My Life in Cricket, Church and the Inner City,* Hodder and Stoughton. Also mentioned in anonymous interview.

51 M. Heseltine (2000) *Life In The Jungle: My Autobiography,* Hodder and Stoughton. Also interviews with R. Key MP and A. Burt MP.

52 See the essays in K. McLoughlin, S. Osborne & E. Fairlie (eds) (2002) *New Public Management – Current Trends and Future Prospects,* Routledge; M. Powell (ed) (1999) *New Labour, New Welfare State – The 'Third Way' in British Social Policy,* Policy Press.

53 P. Taylor Gooby (ed) 2004 *New Risks, New Welfare: The Transformation of the European Welfare State,* Oxford.

productivity' through what became known on mainland Europe as 'the new steering' and in the US as Clinton's 'reinventing government' also emerged.

A watershed moment for traditional social democrats in the UK was the publication in October 1994 of the final report of the Social Justice Commission, which included among its members John (now Bishop) Gladwin.[54] This report declared for the first time for Labour that the purpose of the welfare state was to help economic performance. This had a significant impact on the subsequent development of the 1997 Labour manifesto, and naturally raised a new series of questions about the best way to renew 'governance' and to 'empower' stakeholders to engage in political, civic and democratic processes. This was partly a matter of principle, but it was also an attempt to imagine what the state would look like in a world where the traditional mass produced welfare state was dead.[55]

As John Atherton has put it, 'stakeholding represents a more balanced view of the human than that represented in the old welfare state. Instead of the overemphasis on government welfare as the institutional expression of altruism, there is a recognition of the individual as responsible, driven by proper self-regard or self-interest'.[56] 'Stakeholder welfare' acknowledges the plurality of civil society, the need for partnership between the different sectors in society, and subsidiarity – all of which affirm the indispensability of the contribution of the private and voluntary sectors in welfare delivery. Indeed, the voluntary or 'third' sector is actively encouraged to engage, not simply in 'welfare delivery' but also in the wider project of empowering local communities to develop social capital and establish mechanisms that can promote employment and wellbeing. For segments of the New Labour government, religious groups should be regarded as important participants in these activities. As Elaine Graham has written, the Blairite ideology attempted 'to synthesise the discourse of individualism and personal responsibility with an appeal to localism and subsidiarity as the most effective means of delivering social cohesion'.[57]

Meanwhile, a serious economics of 'well-being' and an articulation of a politics that takes seriously the unspoken vote of future generations and the poorest of the planet in present social accountability[58] have been emerging mostly outside the mainstream

---

54 Commission on Social Justice (1994) *Social Justice: Strategies for National Renewal,* Vintage.

55 Interview: J. Benington.

56 J. Atherton (2000) *Public Theology for Changing Times,* SPCK, p.132.

57 E. Graham (2007) *'Re-thinking the Common Good: Public Theology and the Future of Welfare',* unpublished paper, p.5.

58 For example, P. Dasgupta (2001) *Human Well–Being and the Natural Environment,* Oxford; Also

policy debates. These have been almost absent from mainstream Christian reflection. Although this report is not the place to describe these in detail, we shall address them at greater length in our future work.

2.2 Current Stances on Public Service Reform

Whatever view the Church takes towards the transformation welfare organisation has undergone in the past sixty years, the question it faces is how to respond to the situation *as it is today*. Such a response must first take into account the changing political climate and the stances of both Government and Opposition. Despite many voices in the Church telling us, 'there is no difference between any of the parties on these issues,' the reality is otherwise.

Lisa Harker, co-director of the Institute for Public Policy Research, told us that while all three parties are committed to a strong third sector involvement in social change, the two main parties have deeply contrasting approaches and outlooks rooted in fundamental principles.

Greg Clark MP, Conservative Shadow Minister for Charities, Social Enterprise and Volunteering, seconded this statement. 'The views are quite different... the government is focused on a policy to control and govern the third sector because it is convinced the state alone is the guarantor of justice. This is making it independence averse, risk averse and unwilling to let third sector bodies, including Church groups, do what they are best at or what they value most. Proposals to extend the Human Rights Act would only make this worse'.

2.2.1 Labour - Exit, Voice, and Loyalty

We were told that moves are now well under way within the Labour government to refine what it calls its 'public sector reform strategies'. Crucially, in the light of what we have heard from the Church, this process is informed by a powerful conviction that 'exit, voice and loyalty' (or increased 'choice and governance' as it has been described by others)[59] could help remove blocks to public sector renewal that Labour policy makers see themselves as having encountered, especially in the NHS.[60]

We were told that, partly inspired by Albert Hirschmann's work, Government has sought to introduce 'choice' or flexibility into service provision in order to mirror in

the work of our Von Hügel Institute colleagues Sir Brian Heap FRS and Dr Flavio Comim (www. st-edmunds.cam.ac.uk/vhi/index.shtml).

59   Including several of our interviewees and Lisa Harker of IPPR.

60   J. Benington (ed) 2007 *Reforming Public Services*, HMSO.

the social sector what is said to already occur in the private sector. In Hirschmann's description of the neo-classical market perspective, 'users' or 'customers' of failing organisations send clear signals to them regarding the need for improvement or an organisation's outright failure by withdrawing their custom (i.e. switching to another organisation) when dissatisfied. This can only happen if there are many organisations providing services and products from which 'customers' can choose.[61]

Crucially Hirschmann does not only rely on such a 'classical economic' perspective, but also suggests that key organisational improvements can be influenced by those customers who do not 'exit' immediately and who instead exercise their 'voice' out of a sense of 'loyalty'. In all enterprises, these complaints send a second set of signals to failing organisations regarding the need for renewal. When organisations in the mainstream economy do not respond to either of these sets of feedback, they are likely to collapse.

When applied to government, 'exit, voice and loyalty' seeks to create within public services the range of improvement possibilities upon which market institutions can call. In this view, campaigning, complaining and advocacy are critical for lifting the performance of public services and bureaucracies, many of which are seen to be under pressure in terms of performance. Such advocacy must also sit alongside the introduction of choice to emulate the feedback mechanisms that arise from customers withdrawing from a failing organisation.

In other words, government regards 'advocacy' by civil society groups not as something distinct from 'delivery', but as a fully integrated part of its improvement strategy. 'Advocacy' and 'delivery' are flipsides of the same coin.

For the Church this analysis challenges the 'primacy of prophecy' and advocacy that many at the episcopal and local level told us were starkly different from 'welfare delivery' and ought to be the moral priority of the church because of its 'enhanced radicalism'. In short, civil society – or faith-based - participation in both service delivery and advocacy builds both 'choice' *and* 'voice'. Both are equally valid means by which to improve public sector performance. The Church's understanding would thus seem inadequately nuanced.

Consequently, when the government approaches public sector reform, it does so not with a simple philosophy of 'privatisation' or, it says, by driving commissioning solely on the grounds of 'price'. The combination of 'choice' and 'voice' seeks to introduce

---

61 A. Hirschmann (1970) *Exit, Voice, and Loyalty: Responses to Decline in Firms, Organizations, and States*. Cambridge, MA: Harvard University Press.

a fresh approach that brings the state into full contact with a range of actors who can help it improve, although an instrumental perspective might emerge from this that sees the sole purpose of the third sector as driving public sector improvement. New voices are sought to enter into these conversations, whether they be social entrepreneurs such as Andrew (now Lord) Mawson at the Bromley-by-Bow Centre in London's East End or the community entrepreneurs who have served as community organisers or founded post offices, police stations, and business start-up units within their local church building.

Human Rights and 'The Invasion of Civil Society'

In passing we note that Labour's emphasis on the importance of the state has led it to partially endorse an extension of the classification of 'public authority' throughout the voluntary sector. One Labour MP described this idea as 'reprehensible', while a Conservative thought it 'misjudged'.

This proposal first arose from the cross-party work of the joint Commons and Lords Committee on the 1998 Human Rights Act. The committee was concerned that in the current commissioning/contracting process, the legal duty for the protection of 'human rights' rests with the commissioning body (i.e. a local authority) rather than the providing organisation (i.e. a charity). In the committee's view, this places especially vulnerable users of services at risk of misunderstandings or complex legal processes, and thus of having their rights diluted. The frail users of services seeking to redress human rights grievances would have to sue the 'public authority' who would then have to pursue the 'private' charity. Such a process would demand too much of service users.

Exhortation to the implementation of human rights law by service providers is not working, stated the joint committee, and so they recommend legislation to make private charities 'public bodies', thus ensuring 'the intentions of Parliament' from the time of the Act's passing. Members of the committee have been supported in this stance by some older peoples' organisations and the National Secular Society. If this proposal, now partially endorsed by the Ministry of Justice, succeeds in extending the definition of 'public authority' to service-providing charities, this will fundamentally impact on voluntary sector independence and will likely affect the ethos of Christian organisations. One MP stated that this would mean, 'the effective nationalisation by Government of the civil society sphere'.

This matter of 'public authority' will be revisited in subsequent phases of our work, but at the present time we simply record that the Church of England and the Evangelical

Alliance have vigorously opposed this suggestion. The Church of England's legal advisors are 'surprised that the Charity Commission has done nothing to resist such proposals', and others were 'shocked' that NCVO and other groups had not made more of it either.[62]

2.2.2 Conservatives - Towards 'A Responsible Society'[63]

In July 2007 the Social Justice Policy Group of the Conservative party published a 700 page policy document following a very large scale programme of opinion polling, site visits, project interviews and social research of a task force chaired by Rt Hon Iain Duncan Smith MP.

Greg Clark MP remarked that this document should be considered 'to be as important in terms of a fresh direction for the Conservative party... as the Social Justice Commission of John Smith MP was in the development of a new direction for Labour'.[64]

Such a claim is not unreasonable, as it marks a sharp departure from the party's earlier stances. In the eighties Sir Keith Joseph called social justice a 'will o' the wisp' and in the nineties Dr Robin Harris (former Deputy Director of the Downing Street Policy Unit) castigated monasteries for their egalitarian habit of sharing.[65] At an IEA seminar attended by one of the authors in the early nineties, Michael Novak (American Enterprise Institute) received great applause for denigrating social justice as 'just another word for envy'. Yet more recently, the chief executive of a prominent Christian charity told us 'that the new breed of Conservative that comes to my homelessness charity are different. There is a genuine thirst to understand and combat poverty'.

The Conservatives' Social Justice report is indeed stridently anti-poverty, but what is notable is that it suggests most particularly that poverty is being driven by a breakdown in the 'social fabric' of the UK.[66] It laments the manner in which Britain 'has become materially more prosperous', yet this increased wealth has not alleviated many 'social problems'. 'Vast amounts' have been spent on public services with little effect, and 'rates of family breakdown, educational failure, economic dependency, addictions

---

62 *The Meaning of Public Authority Under The Human Rights Act* (2007) House of Lords/House of Commons Joint Committee on Human Rights Ninth Report of Session 2006-07, HMSO.

63 D. Cameron (2007) *Social Responsibility - The Big Idea for Britain's Future*, Conservative Party.

64 Interview with G. Clark MP, April 2008.

65 R. Harris op cit.

66 *Breakthrough Britain - Ending Costs of Social Breakdown* (2007) Social Justice Policy Group, Conservative Party; Interview with G. Clark MP.

and serious personal debt' have remained 'stubbornly high'. In contrast to Labour, the Conservatives' report argues that renewal will come, not through public sector action and reform but by 'liberating the third sector from the incessant pressure to do the government's work in the government's way'. For the Conservatives, a responsible and cohesive society is the guarantor of justice, not the state.

At this point, it is worth quoting the 'modern' Conservative mission in full to gain a better picture of their aims.

> To fight social injustice and help the most disadvantaged by building a strong society. The test of a strong and just society is how it looks after the least advantaged – but this duty is *not reserved for the state alone*. It is a *shared responsibility*: we are all in this together. [67] (emphasis ours)

Of especial interest to this study are a few of the subsequent goals pertaining to the third sector.

- Setting social enterprises and the voluntary sector free to tackle multiple deprivation through long-term funding, increased scope to innovate and a level playing field with the public sector.

- Enabling the voluntary sector to create a national programme for young people to support their personal development and promote a sense of social responsibility as they move from childhood to adult life.

- Measures, including clearer rights to respite care, to recognise the role played by voluntary carers, without whom local social services would be wholly incapable of meeting the needs of the disabled and the chronically ill.

In pursuit of a more independent and responsive voluntary sector, the Conservatives are troubled by what they see as the bureaucratisation of the sector and are 'gravely concerned' that this has led to a situation under Labour where '70% of total (charitable) income is generated by just 2% of the sector' and 18 mega charities 'have come to corner… one eighth of the sector's income'. This trend is driven by two factors: the inability of smaller local charities to compete with larger charities to raise voluntary income and the nature of government contracts that favour very large organisations. Furthermore, certain 'favoured' organisations have benefitted more than others under the current government.

According to Opposition, this in turn causes profound civic failure, because these two trends stifle local voluntary sector innovation and creativity. The Conservatives

---

67 Conservative Party (2006) *Built To Last*. Downloaded (20th Feb 2008) at www.conservatives.com

aim to support national initiatives that emphasise *local action*. They also focus on incentives and outcomes rather than on what they describe as the government's overemphasis on specifications of process and results in commissioning regimes. The Conservative rhetoric is consistent with a positive attempt to respond to the concerns aired by all of our Church respondents that charities should be independent, funded in the long term and able to develop innovatively without over-regulation.

In practice, they propose naming certain areas of urban social exclusion 'Social Enterprise Zones' with tax incentives to encourage investment. Other ideas include exposing all year six pupils to the habit of giving by presenting them each with £5 to donate to a charity, and increased monitoring and central action to make sure that local authorities are forced to develop more responsive funding frameworks locally. There are also proposals to encourage local volunteering, giving and participation, as well as a call to decentralise contracting in order to increase the number of third sector bodies able and willing to have 'more resources channelled' to them to 'tackle poverty'. Continuing the emphasis on autonomy in the sector, there is also a commitment to make it easier to transfer un- or under-used public/state assets to local community organisations to endow them and reduce drastically the over-specification of contracts, which diminishes voluntary sector innovation. Meanwhile, central government funding should be focused not on a national elite of third sector bodies, but should be aimed at building up local Community Foundations via the use of a National Challenge Fund.[68] These policies will form the context for a new Voluntary Sector green paper to be published in late 2008.

Of all our interviewees, Conservative advisors and politicians were among the most comfortable and enthusiastic regarding involving faith groups in this renewal of the third sector, and believed that Christian churches had something 'unique' to bring to the table as strong local leaders. This enthusiasm is reiterated in *Breakthrough Britain* and in formal policy documents. Conservative reports explicitly acknowledge that Christian groups are being 'discriminated' against at the local level in their attempts to contribute to society and suggest new legislation to deal with this problem.

It is important to note that much of this enthusiasm in the Conservative party arises from evidence of, and reflection on, the contributions of black evangelical churches in inner city areas.[69] Such a focus runs the risk of underestimating the significance of Anglican buildings to suburban and rural areas and of Diocesan bodies and

---

68 *Breakthrough Britain* op cit; interview with Greg Clark MP.
69 Interview, Centre for Social Justice.

cathedrals, which can enrich local roots. It also risks making normative judgements rooted in analysis in only one form of religious denomination.

As we have said the Conservative Commission on Social Justice believes that 'new legislation should be introduced to put faith groups on a level playing field', but also that a 'faith standard' should be created so that religious organisations can have their services benchmarked against objective standards. It is interesting that the Department of Communities and Local Government has subsequently adopted this proposal, and at the time of our writing is consulting on the possibility of using something akin to the Faithworks Charter as its 'standard' (Appendix A).[70]

2.2.3 In Sum

It is not the purpose of this report to analyse fully the shifting sands of either party's policy positions, nor is it our role to say which party most reflects a Christian ideal or a preferred policy option. Nonetheless, it is essential for Anglicans to engage deeply with both of these policy paradigms, for neither reflects the perceptions about the direction of policy development that we have encountered in the Church and its networks.

Conceivably this shortcoming arises from the absence of a detailed theology of 'public management' among Christians. Political theologies have focused on inputs to the state and its outputs, but not on the process of priority setting.[71] The 'scarring political battles' of the eighties are over, and a new nuanced language of policy, governance, participation and justice has emerged with an increased emphasis throughout civil society on professionalism and attention to detail. Somehow modern theological reflection needs to engage with this agenda.[72]

---

70 *Face to Face* op cit. The DCLG's final policies/guidance in this area are awaited at the time of going to press.

71 F. Davis (Jan 2005) 'No More Tax And Spend' *The Tablet*. Downloadable at http://new.youngfoundation.org/node/265

72 In our interviews, for example, we frequently encountered the view that all 'management' came from the private sector and was focused on 'profit'. Furthermore, 'states' were all viewed as the same and had similar 'duties'. In sharp contrast, literature on family enterprise, non-profit management, cultural variations in markets, the metaphors of organisation and charity law contest this perspective. See, for example, G. Morgan (1986) *Images Of Organisation* Sage; S.G. Redding (1990) *The Spirit of Chinese Capitalism* De Gruyter; P. Six & A. Randon (1995) *Liberty, Charity and Politics: Non Profit Law and Freedom of Speech* Dartmouth.

2.3 Are All 'Contracts' the Same?

In stark contrast to this nuanced policy view, we frequently encountered the belief from individuals in the Church that there is a single, normative, 'contracting' regime, which does and would define all relationships between the Church, the wider voluntary sector and the state. It is on the basis of this view that many smaller Church groups, especially at the parish and deanery level, are intensely critical of 'outsourcing' and 'doing the government's job' after they struggled with contracting and consistent hostility on the part of the local government. These same small groups often have the ear of the concerned episcopacy and inform episcopal reservations regarding the 'commissioning state', where such reservations exist.

Many within the Church feel that they are 'the local authority's last port of call… the place they come to when no one else will touch a project or a need… in the hope that we can sort it for them'. This is not experienced as partnership but 'exploitation'. We fully acknowledge these frustrations on the part of the Church, but also want to observe that it is problematic to leap from these perspectives to a total critique of government commissioning – unless one starts from a foundational position that the state should own and directly deliver all services.

We interviewed the leaders and managers of several larger Christian voluntary sector bodies about their experience of negotiating contracts and service level agreements. We also spoke to some managers in the secular third sector. In both cases mention was made that local authorities vary widely in the way that they go about purchasing and commissioning. Some seem to be very flexible and understand voluntary sector needs, while others delay payments (putting organisations under pressure) and need every detail spelled out for them.

The clerical CEO of an award–winning social enterprise said:

> We have some contracts which come in "blocks" and guarantee a certain level of income for a certain level of activity providing social care… but we also have contracts where we have negotiated ourselves onto the provider list, and we are one of about four different agencies that the local authority will call on a "spot" basis to undertake social care tasks for various frail older people. We suspect that some purchasing allocations are influenced by private sector hospitality budgets despite the presence of rigorous policies to constrain that sort of thing.

The biggest challenge he faces is not contracting in itself, but the local authority's IT set-up, which makes it difficult for the purchasing local manager to record how many spot purchases of social care they have made. Hence, the social enterprise had to support the local authority's administrative weakness – at some cost to itself – without being able to charge for it![73]

Consistency of cash flow was also a problem that plagued many of our interviewees, rather than contracts as such. Although the Treasury has agreed three year funding rounds with local authorities, the move in social care towards individual delegated budgets to be used totally at the discretion of individuals in need will likely provoke a new series of demands regarding income and cash flow that many organisations have never faced before.[74] Even here there is huge variation, as some voluntary sector organisations have negotiated with local authorities and primary care trusts to receive payment up to a quarter in advance.

We encountered strong feelings that the Voluntary Sector Compact was unlikely to help in this regard and may even 'be a distraction'. As one CEO told us:

> If the Voluntary Sector Compact is supposed to be the answer to this problem, then that is just another function of civil servants not understanding the lack of relationship in the real world between cost-price and value when you have a portfolio of activities, that overhead recovery becomes more complex the more "jobbing" is the nature of the work, and that if you have 700 staff to look after you need to balance all of this with operational systems and approaches that some very traditional professions find challenging… If Government outsources a service and then ties us up in inflexibility, then why bother? Full cost recovery is a function of size, operational innovation and pricing, not bureaucratic judgement.[75]

Faithworks told us that a motivating factor to diversify into the Academies programme was the search for consistent cash flow and funding to underpin wider activities. 'We signed a 25-year contract,' said Steve Chalke, 'and that's what the Church of England's Academies will all be doing'. Faithworks is now looking at the health sector because of similar opportunities for sustainability. GP practices, for example, come with very long term contracts against which it is possible to borrow start up and development funds (even if fixed NHS tariff prices are causing a huge strain in areas of poverty where poor people need multiple appointments to resolve neglected needs, but GPs are funded only on a single tariff allocation). Some NHS dental contracts are also in this position, especially in areas where NHS dentistry

---

73 Interview.
74 Voluntary Sector Compact (www.thecompact.org.uk).
75 Interview.

has been highly underdeveloped and new NHS entrants have to deal with years of neglect.[76]

While we found many in the Church who expressed strong views on 'contracting', we found far fewer who were aware of mainstream economic predictions that 'public sector markets' are set to grow [77] or who fully appreciated how extensive state purchasing power is. From school food provision to printing for the Ministry of Defence, from training for the unemployed to ministerial transport by plane, from the purchase of weapons to the financing of hospitals and the delivery of overseas aid and development in Africa, from the provision of village halls to the funding of motorways, from research to toilet cleaning, from estate management to logistics – the lines between what is 'state' and 'private' have been radically blurred in every department of state.

This is not to deny that problems of short-termism exist in commissioning. We simply want to record the strongly held view that we encountered in larger bodies that the key questions are of 'understanding, trust, the form of the contract, capacity and negotiation, negotiation and negotiation again'.

We were told that the Department for Work and Pensions, for example, had decided to pursue the creation of huge 'head' contracts for the provision of welfare-to-work, which would then involve the lead provider in sub-contracting to other parties, including voluntary sector bodies. Large regional contracts for the provision of probation were also the policy proposal associated with the early stages of the National Offender Management Services. Strong concerns were expressed that this approach would exclude even very experienced voluntary sector bodies. One very successful person-centred agency, Ascend in Hertfordshire, believed this direction in policy to be positively *anti*-voluntary sector and representative of a 'lack of understanding of the multi-dimensional needs of those who are really struggling'.

At the BBC we heard of past use of 'reverse auctions' where jobs were awarded on the basis of the organisation that bids the lowest price, forcing competing providers to bid increasingly lower.

For Faithworks, there is a concern that the development of a faith charter says nothing about 'the reciprocal responsibilities of government to be reasonable, to have standards, which might include breaking contracts into sizes and forms across

76 Interview Brian Strevens.
77 G. Mulgan (2007) in Benington(ed) op cit.

regions, localities and even nationally which would then allow third sector bodies, including the churches, to be in a position to bid on a more level playing field'.

Best Practice and the Dangers of 'Service On The Cheap'

While it is essential to note that blanket observations about the nature of 'contracts' do not adequately tease out variations across regions, or even the same department, concerns about commissioning 'services on the cheap' consistently featured in our feedback.

Despite the good intentions of 'Best Value' criteria, we heard that it was proving 'necessary' for purchasers to interpret these in their narrowest sense in pursuit of savings and short-term viability. One Primary Care Trust purchasing director told us that she had to focus on cost and that the 'form of the organisation was irrelevant in the face of such pressure. Just because the organisation is local, or a charity, or non-profit will not do,' she said, 'I have no slack to give them leeway'.

A few interviewees told us that such best practices already existed in some places, but were not being replicated across the welfare state. Many told us that a new statement of principles as to what might constitute the appropriate ethics of government commissioning would be a significant step forward.

Later in the report we outline some emerging Christian principles on contracting that draw upon the feedback we received.

2.4 The Risk of Self-Referential Radicalism

As stated previously, during our interviews and consultations we encountered Christian individuals and groups with an instinctively negative reaction to the concept of church-based organisations becoming involved in 'the contract culture'. They believed firmly that the Church's calling was to the task of advocacy and 'prophecy', not 'service delivery on behalf of the government', and discerned a clear moral distinction between the two. Ironically, from the perspective of a government operating within an 'exit, voice and loyalty' framework, such advocacy directly contributes to its programme of public service reform, with the Church finding itself inside an 'improvement loop' and not, as it might imagine, standing against the 'dominant culture'.

Those arguing the 'prophecy' case included the bishop who, as we have said, saw the commissioning state as a 'cross-party plot' along with the majority of community based activists and development workers we interviewed or met. A number quoted writers such as Stanley Hauerwas[78] to argue that it is not the Church's job to be 'useful' but to witness 'prophetically' to a 'distinctive narrative'. Others, influenced by 'liberation' and other theologies that claim to emphasise 'community' above 'competition', cited the need to struggle for 'kingdom values' of justice and equality (of outcome) to be reflected in society. However, their responses tended to be extremely vague when asked what this meant in terms of practical policy (e.g. it might lead to launching a campaign) or what they would ask Anglicans to do to realise such rhetoric. The 'moral supremacy' of advocacy was also articulated in some parts of the wider voluntary sector with whom we spoke, especially smaller members of NCVO.

It is important to note that many of these voices often intended something more 'radical' than mere lobbying. 'Prophetic', in their usage, relates less to predicting the future than to articulating the perceived mind of God and confronting 'authorities' and the populace with 'uncomfortable truths' about contemporary events and trends, which they judge to be unacceptable. The Hebrew Bible (Old Testament) contains many striking examples of prophets speaking in 'judgement' against rulers, and it could be argued that New Testament figures such as John the Baptist and Jesus of Nazareth also fulfilled such a prophetic ministry. While prophets claim to speak 'for God', they may also claim to represent the interests of those lacking the power to shape their own lives.

In today's context this would arguably include many recipients of welfare or those experiencing some other form of social exclusion. Prophetic statements, in addition to possibly challenging the status quo, may offer alternative visions of society. Such visions, though, will only have impact if they are grounded in a sound analysis of the social, economic and political dynamic of the situation being addressed. Some of the rhetoric we encountered in sections of the Church about government officials, members of professions, trade unions, voluntary agencies and 'the poor' being 'always virtuous', while business leaders, entrepreneurs, and public managers never can be, clearly lacks such realistic grounding. It also unreflectively avoids any deep understanding of human motivation, agency and action,[79] let alone a nuanced theology of 'sin'.

With this in mind it is notable that we repeatedly heard from those who are successfully influencing the Government's and Opposition's agenda that the era of the 'simple speech, statement or lecture' as a means of advancing social change is over. 'We live

---

78 For example, S. Hauerwas (1981) *A Community of Character,* Notre Dame.

79 J. Le Grand (2003) *Motivation, Agency and Public Policy – Of Knights, Knaves, Pawns and Queens,* Oxford.

in a world which is interested in those that can *deliver*,' said one leading Christian CEO. Another asserted that agencies 'influence service design and the shape of policy by engaging in the commissioning and delivery process'. A former Downing Street senior staffer told us, 'the best way to get change is to establish pioneering work and then see that it is visited by senior people and replicated thereafter'. Interestingly, not a single parliamentarian that we spoke to thought that the Church should not engage in public service reform, although in some cases this view was expressed with a degree of caution. In a few cases the enthusiasm was overwhelming.

The implications of these insights are significant, because they point towards another set of judgements; namely, who are the most appropriate people within the Church to take on particular roles. Key questions to ponder in this respect:

- Is the advocacy of a bishop more or less compelling when it comes to social change than that of a Christian CEO of a pioneering community project or social enterprise?

- Is the fundraising 'ask' of a bishop more or less persuasive to donors than that of the same Christian CEO?

- Should community-based projects (and parishes) – which may have a turnover of less than £100,000 - be contemplating taking on contracts of an equivalent or larger scale?

- To what extent are those that claim to be prophetic just part of a public service reform process, reliant on the very culture that they claim to resist for the space to 'witness'; perhaps consequently lacking any radicalism at all?

Arguably, the judgement for the Church of England to make is not a blanket one between engaging with a so-called 'marketising strategy' that is 'morally unacceptable' and an advocacy strategy that is 'morally pure', or between 'public sector virtues' and 'private sector vices'. Rather, the Church will need to shape appropriate priorities and strategies in different contexts and different regions in the light of theological reflection, prayer and informed social analysis. This might include seeking enhanced autonomy as well as increased engagement with the state. But whatever strategies it adopts, the capacity and skills that the Church is able to draw upon will be crucial. It is to these issues that we shall shortly turn.

2.5 A Crisis of Government Evidence and Conversation

While Christians seek to draw principles for action from Scripture, preaching and tradition ('what matters'), modern governments depend on 'evidence- based policy'

- an approach that claims to focus on 'what works'. However, a closer inspection of the ethics, values and principles informing many policy choices and positions suggests that they are, as we have touched upon, rooted in a profound understanding of what constitutes human flourishing.[80]

Articulating the relationship between 'what matters' and 'what works' for Christians has never been easy. All of our faith-based respondents reported 'immense religious illiteracy' on the part of local government officials, politicians and throughout the policy-making community as a whole. As we have said, the view most consistently expressed was that all faiths were 'private ideas' or 'private practices' with relevance only on one day of the week. This contrasted with a 'gut feeling' expressed in other quarters that the Church 'is doing a lot around the place'.

Prevalent also was a misinformed belief that across the board 'Christian churches are declining and relying on ageing white women for their numbers'. Dioceses such as London and Southwark, which have enjoyed an increase in Church attendance and an internationalisation of congregations, would seem to refute such a claim. It is also a statistically contested area of forecasting.[81]

Notwithstanding these comments, we were astonished to be told by civil servants that there is no evidence base in government circles on Christian institutions. Indeed, in some quarters the very idea that such an evidence base may be relevant to a modern social or policy agenda seemed fantastic. Yet we are aware of specially commissioned government studies on minority faiths, extensive work on Muslim 'radicalisation' and research into specific (black) evangelical churches. Not surprisingly, as we suggested above, we heard that some minority faiths felt 'under surveillance'.

The government itself has commented that the data on the non-profit sector from the Office for National Statistics (ONS) does not serve the sector well,[82] and NCVO has called data on religion 'limited' at best.[83] ONS data on the churches is weak because it is presented in terms of 'average numbers of believers' rather than acknowledging regional nuance. Based on our interviews with politicians, government officials and people in the faith communities themselves, we can only conclude that the absence of a 'churches' evidence base is grounded in a judgement that churches are not worthy to

---

80 J. Le Grand op cit; R. Plant (1991) *Modern Political Thought*, Blackwells.

81 Interview with Rev Lynda Barley.

82 Cabinet Office (2007) Background Document for Tender (with Barrow Cadbury Trust) to Provide Expert Evidence Based Centre on the Third Sector.

83 O. Reichardt et al (2008) *The UK Civil Society Almanac* NCVO.

have even a modest role in government schemes. Such a judgement contrasts strongly with public declarations by Ministers that all of civil society is welcome to the public service reform table and that the government's agenda is for all faiths rather than for a few. Yet if what we were told is correct, the churches simply do not register on the policy-making radar in serious terms, despite the best efforts of some excellent Ministers and MPs.[84]

Crucially for government, the absence of an evidence base on the Christian churches means that it has been planning blindly in the third sector. The Charity Commission's data on the size, scope and nature of faith-based/religious charities in general is *profoundly flawed*, and the government has focused its evidence gathering so intensely on minority faiths that it has failed to develop a coherent evidence base for the largest religious body – and one of the largest third sector players - in the UK, the Christian church.

It would be surprising if this failure were not causing management problems for the state at the level of national and local government. For those Christian charity executives that we interviewed, *theology* is the very organisational theory according to which they discern and arrange their strategies and performance criteria. Even at the level of organisational analysis, discounting this theological underpinning out of hand – as some in politics, government and voluntary sector umbrella bodies clearly do – is equivalent to saying that the BBC's adoption of 'public value' criteria for the campaign to renew its licence, or a private sector organisation's harnessing of the 'excellence' model, is not relevant for understanding its practical strategies. Such an understanding of 'theology' may be key to teasing out how 'fit for purpose' the organisation is when it comes to the allocation of state resources.

2.6 Problems at the Charity Commission and Beyond

In 2007 the Charity Commission judged itself to have completed a highly successful three-year consultation process with the faith communities.[85] This programme of work drew heavily on the faith and social cohesion unit at the DCLG and on specialist advice from the Foreign Office. It led to the creation of a new Charity Commission Faith and Cohesion Unit, which 'would focus on the Muslim community in the first instance'.

---

84 We found consistently positive feedback regarding the work of Rt Hon John Battle MP and Rt Hon Stephen Timms MP in particular.

85 *Working With Faith Groups: The Charity Commission Faith Groups Programme 2004-07.* Downloadable at www.charity-commission.gov.uk/enhancingcharities/faithgroup.asp

In its report published in December 2007 the Charity Commission said that it had become interested in faith-based charities (i.e. advancing religion) for a variety of reasons, but focused its attention on independent evangelical Christian congregations and mosques. This led it to initiate a new three-year engagement that involved most of the UK's minority faiths because the Commission believed that, 'although these faiths are classed as minority in the UK, we were sensitive to the fact that they include the main worldwide religions'. In global terms the accuracy of this claim is unclear, but in either event it positively excluded the two largest religious groupings in the country, the Church of England and the Roman Catholic Church!

The Commission claimed that as a result of the 'new research' conducted during its three-year consultation, it had unearthed 'in excess of 25,500 faith-based charities'. However, in a report published around the same time, the Carnegie Commission into the Future of Civil Society claimed to have been told by the Charity Commission that there were 23,383 charities registered by religion with a total income of £4.6 billion. The Carnegie Commission observes that this must be an understatement because the figure did not include Church of England parishes whose number is in excess of 16,000![86] Even the NCVO's *Civil Society Almanac* - described by Minister for the Third Sector, Ed Miliband, as 'the sector's most important reference book' – is deficient. Although the *Almanac* is an important resource for evidence-based debates on policy in particular and for NCVO's advocacy of the sector in general, its ability to record the size of the 'faith sector' is limited.

When we met with senior figures within NCVO, they reiterated the view that 'faith' needed to be integrated more into the mainstream sector, the trouble being that 'faith sees itself as a separate realm'. We were thus unsurprised that several Christian voluntary bodies told us that they only felt genuinely welcome at the Association of Chief Executives of Voluntary Organisations (ACEVO).

Based on its impressions of faith, the March 2008 NCVO *Almanac* stated that there were 10,213 faith-based charities on the register in 2005/6 with an income of £3.19 billion and assets of £11.9 billion. The *Almanac* judged that the requirement in the new Charity Act for 'excepted charities' with a gross income exceeding £100,000 to report to the Commission would mean that 2,734 more faith-based charities would be added to the Charity Commission's statistics from 1 October 2008.

---

86 Inquiry into the Future of Civil Society in UK and Ireland (2007) *The Shape of Civil Society To Come*, Carnegie Trust.

This confusion surrounding the number of faith-based charities, particularly Anglican ones, has a long history. In the initial preparation for what became the Charity Act of 2006, the Government's own strategy unit pointed out that the Charity Commission's classification criteria led it significantly to understate the number of black and minority ethnic (BME) community voluntary organisations. Quoting a complementary study, they reported that as many as 18% of BME organisations were faith-based. It could be inferred that the number of faith groups is being misstated.[87]

More worryingly, Elizabeth Palmer has argued that this underestimation due to failures of classification and understanding runs much deeper.[88] Researching on the Charity Commission's website, Palmer noted that charities are classified by their type of beneficiary, their function or their field of operation. Consequently, she spent time searching the database by name, registration number, areas in which charities worked and by key words. Based on the names of charities and their objects she judged that five out of eight organisations in her research cohort would not have been classified as 'religious' or 'faith-based' despite the fact that they were fully and self consciously Christian in origin, ethos and governance. Fearing that this may be a misperception she contacted the Charity Commission helpdesk, and her discovery was verified. Palmer comments that if her findings are representative in the social welfare sector then the faith-based charity population on the Charity Commission's register alone 'would be understated by as much as 62.5%'.

Using the same method we searched the Charity Commission's website. We discovered that the Bishop of Guildford's Foundation, Church Action on Poverty, Housing Justice, The Passage Centre for the Homeless, Methodist Homes for the Aged, several Catholic children's societies, and the St Vincent de Paul Society would not count as religious charities, despite their expressed ethos, constituencies and titles! Even Islamic Relief, described by the DCLG as 'the largest Muslim charity in the UK', would not count as a faith-based organisation for the Charity Commission because it did not expressly state 'advancing religion' in its objects. On telephoning the Charity Commission ourselves in February 2008, we had this perception confirmed. In such circumstances it is unsurprising how enduring Cabinet office and central government misperceptions and prejudices are.

It could be argued that a classification of 'ethos' may be interesting, but would not add anything to policy understanding or change the charity's 'activities'. The problem arises

87 See Strategy Unit (2002) *Private Action, Public Benefit* and associated discussion documents downloadable at www.number10.gov.uk.

88 E. Palmer (2008) *The True Cost of Sustainable Funding*, Unpublished thesis, South Bank University.

that the Christian chief executives who we interviewed explicitly viewed 'theology' as their theory of organisation and their priority setting framework. In their minds, Government's decision to ignore theology as a governance criterion means that the *state* has delineated what constituted 'good' religion and asserted that faith did not impact on organisational behaviour. Furthermore, this viewpoint privatised the public consequences of religious ideas. 'This', said one respondent, "is disrespectful, discriminatory and shortsighted".

The other challenge is that if a weak set of classification criteria downgrades the enormous civic contribution of a vital national community, then Government risks making misjudged strategic attempts at support. The Church Urban Fund's surveys suggest that Anglican bodies turn to umbrella networks in their own community before calling on one of the secular umbrella bodies.[89] This largely happens because many of the secular institutions were seen to be religion averse and/or inexperienced in the governance strategies of faith-based organisations.

When it comes to teasing out the full extent of Anglican civic action, it is also important to note that even if we included 'faith-based charities that are on the Commission's register, this would still exclude Anglican parishes or other Christian bodies with charitable status by exception or exemption. For example, the Church of England's Stewardship Office estimates that around 14,000 'excepted' parishes will not have to report to the Commission under the new Charity Act, even though many will have incomes of £90,000 or more. Meanwhile, Anglican schools, universities and various other bodies are not yet fully covered by such provisions, although this will change for many in 2009.

This in turn raises questions as to the regional definitions of what constitutes 'the charitable' and the nature of the voluntary sector. Further on in this report, we will point to the huge array of activities going on in parishes and other Anglican bodies in the Midlands and North. Very often these activities are located in 'excepted' organisations that Charity Commission categorisations do not capture as faith-based voluntary organisations or even as charities. Combined with the high levels of Christian religious conviction shown in the North in the 2001 Census data, it is conceivable that a missing link in the measurement of the civic health of the North are those activities which take place in, through and from the churches. This would be a counterweight to NCVO's current view that most voluntary activity is currently concentrated in the South. In this regard it will be important for Church leaders to

---

89 Interview at Church Urban Fund.

track research funded by the Northern Rock Foundation currently being undertaken by Professor John Mohan of Southampton University on the sector in the North East, as it will likely have wider implications.

These different definitions and understandings of faith-based organisations may be legitimate perceptions of sections of some religious communities, but they do not appreciate the profound reality that the Christian churches are engaged in every single part of 'civil society'. In the UK one can find the following, which have been founded, inspired and run by the Church of England and other Christian denominations:

- Co-operatives
- Universities
- Housing associations
- Independent schools
- Building societies
- Common investment funds
- Industrial and provident and friendly societies
- Benevolent societies
- Museums
- Informal Community Organisations
- Parent Teachers Associations
- Credit Unions

Despite this reality, the NCVO almanac lists all of these categories, yet confines faith-based groups to 'other' rather than seamlessly flagging them as being present across all of the categories where they properly belong.[90]

On the basis of our interviews and research, the absence of evidence on the part of the government has serious ramifications. We were repeatedly told that the perceived experience of certain minority religious communities had been extrapolated to inform normative policy recommendations and frameworks for *all* religious bodies, effectively ignoring the larger communities with greater civic capacity, social capability and community assets.

While we rejoice that the Commission and Government have entered into conversation with minority faiths, we also judge that the omission that we have described raises

---

90 Reichardt et al, op cit.

doubts about the quality of the Commission's relationship with the *whole* realm of religious Britain in particular and the third sector in general, not to mention about the expressed priorities of its new Faith and Social Cohesion Unit. If minority faiths are not to feel victimised and other faiths discriminated against, this needs to be corrected.

Furthermore, the Charity Commission's view, as demonstrated in its guidance on public benefit, as to what constitutes 'the advancement of religion' or a 'faith-based charity' has little or no relation to the way that many people of faith actually understand their way of life or the embodiment of their religious principles in personal volunteering and the creation of institutions. For example, the work of cathedrals is self-defined by a deep understanding of the idea of 'hospitality', which includes educational, cultural, and other activities that are not flagged aggressively as 'religious'. Therefore, to subdivide the charitable activities of a cathedral into the 'religious' as opposed to the educational, cultural and other would be to rewrite its theology. It would mean that the Commission would make the judgements as to what constitutes good religion despite protestations to the contrary.

Moreover, the Commission's recent guidance[91] specifically states that activities which might harm the 'national interest' or which include quoting sacred texts to advance a political purpose are no longer to be judged as 'advancing religion'. It would seem that this idea of 'national interest' is a strange extension of the traditional idea of 'harmful' religion, and yet it is inadequately defined. Such a stance would have neutered St Paul's Cathedral's funding of the legal defence funds for Nelson Mandela, and currently it would emasculate much evangelical work to defend persecuted minorities in Burma and South Asia whose plight has been particularly highlighted by the Conservative Party's Human Rights Commission. We note that Greg Clark MP is aware of this issue and 'watching it with interest'.

While the Commission views its position as being rooted in case law, the key question will be the leeway with which it approaches these matters. The Conservative proposal for new legislation to protect faith groups from discrimination in the public welfare realm could be a basis on which to correct faulty case law when it does not accurately reflect social reality.

With these points in mind we concur with the Carnegie Commission, which called for more research on the faith sector to quantify its size and contribution. We go further

---

91 Charity Commission (Feb 2008) *Charities And Public Benefit – The Charity Commission's General Guidance on Public Benefit* and *Draft Supplementary Guidance on Advancement of Religion.*

in saying that the current situation risks the exclusion of the Church of England from a series of regional and national debates, and leads to regional policy makers acting on less than robust evidence from the Charity Commission in particular. In turn we observe that this is now beginning to contribute to weaknesses in policy design that may actually undermine civic health.

It is without a doubt the case that the government is fundamentally underestimating the number of Christian charities to the tune of thousands, and consequently their social, economic and civic impact and potential. At the least this means that the government cannot include this contribution in its deliberations. At most this raises again the view asserted by so many of our respondents, 'This Government is positively excluding people of faith'.

A Note on Religious Assets

In passing we wish to note that the underestimation of the number of Anglican charities is likely to lead many surveys to underestimate their financial and asset contribution as well. The true market value of churches and other properties is hard to determine, especially when they are carried (if at all) in balance sheets at their book value, and may include a car park and/or surrounding land as well as the church building itself.

This trend may be extended to the issue of schools and into other Christian denominations. For example, the assets of Roman Catholic voluntary aided schools are very rarely included in Diocesan balance sheets, because a partial payment would be due from and to the government in the event of their sale and because it is hard to apply the value of 'planning gain' potential to an operating school. Moreover, in some situations the application of Roman Catholic canon law to the closure of certain enclosed religious houses/monasteries (which are *not* charitable) requires that the bulk of the sale proceeds should revert to the local diocese (which *is* charitable) where the enclosed house is located. In practice, this pattern suggests likely significant off-balance sheet assets in more than one denominational structure. This pattern may be repeated among charities where Sharia law is a governance factor in trustee decision-making. It is certainly a factor in Anglican accounting where currently consecrated land is not required to be included in balance sheets.

PART 3: CAPABILITY AND STRUCTURE: TOWARDS AN EVIDENCE BASE

We have noted that Government's evidence regarding religious bodies, in so far as it exists, tends to concentrate on the congregational level. We have also noted that within such a framework, Government and the Charity Commission vastly underestimate the extent of Anglican 'congregational' existence.

In this section we turn to institutional forms of theological significance in Anglican life (dioceses, cathedrals), not least as they represent religious bodies, which already have found meaningful ways of partnering with state funders. These structures also have been largely absent from government evidence and strategic policy design.

3.1 Diocesan Survey

To discern the Church's civic potential, we needed to move beyond 'congregations' as the primary defining structural characteristic of religious analysis. Therefore, in the autumn of 2007 we undertook an empirical study of all Church of England dioceses. 28 of the 44 dioceses returned the surveys, a 64% response rate.

The purpose of the survey was to assess the current capacity of the dioceses in terms of human and financial resources, as well as to determine what experience diocesan employees had with contracting.

For clarity it is important to note that in the Anglican Church, diocesan assets and staffing are distinct from parish resources. The Roman Catholic Church, on the other hand, often consolidates parish income and assets into a single Diocesan charity number for reasons of financial efficiency while simultaneously maintaining parish autonomy under canon law. This structural distinction undermines some studies, which argue that these two Churches are directly comparable for civil society analysis purposes because they 'share a parochial structure'. We state this clearly here as some research projects have conflated these two large denominations for analytical purposes.[92]

3.1.1 Financial Resources

We discovered that while some dioceses experience tight cash flows and profit and loss account deficits, the majority do not. All dioceses reported positive net assets/reserves

---

92 This claim has been made by the UK wing of a Ford Foundation study on international religious bodies located at Roehampton University. Quoted in F. Davis et al (2006) *The Ground of Justice,* Von Hügel Institute.

using their current book value (Chart 1). It is highly likely that the current market value of assets in some dioceses is higher than reported here, although with varying numbers of listed buildings and asset mixes, this is hard to predict without further exploration.

Chart 1. Assets/Reserves of the Surveyed dioceses (£)

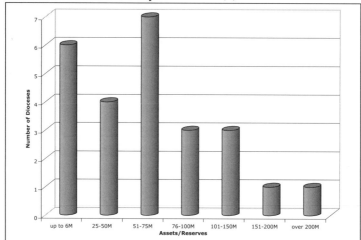

11 dioceses currently provide social welfare services resourced by state funding. Only 2 dioceses receiving state funding for welfare services reported unrestricted income of over £10 million. For comparison, 6 dioceses who are not providing welfare services have indicated income of over £10M. (7 dioceses did not reply to this question.) In total 9 dioceses indicated a reported loss (Chart 2).

Chart 2. Surplus/Loss Levels of Surveyed dioceses

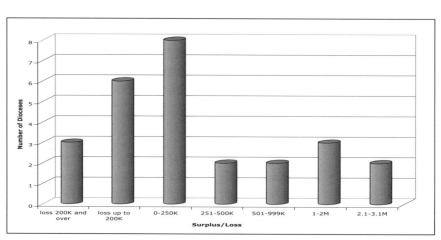

Of the 9 dioceses reporting losses, 5 currently receive state funding for welfare provision. This means almost 50% of the dioceses engaged in contracts with the government are operating on a loss. Furthermore, only 5 contracting dioceses have reported a surplus compared to 12 that are not currently contracting.

Chart 3. Cash Flow of Surveyed dioceses (£)

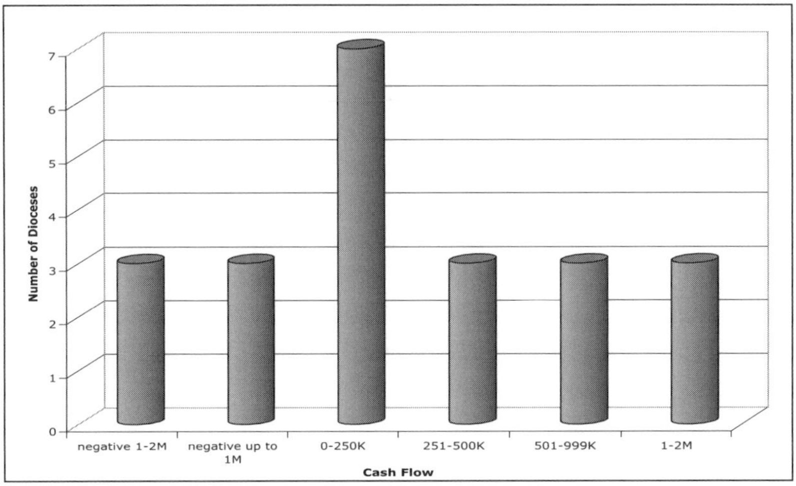

6 dioceses in total reported a negative cash flow (Chart 3).

3 of these 6 dioceses currently provide welfare services resourced by state funding, with the same number not engaged yet.

Of those reporting a positive cash flow, a much higher number (11) were not contracting with the state than were (only 5). Perhaps one reason for this seeming mismatch between resources and action is the anticipation of difficulties expressed by some dioceses engaged in welfare service provision. Responses to the question about problems such dioceses are experiencing included: 'European funding: complex time consuming monitoring, retrospective payment', 'cash flow [problem] because of no upfront funding', 'Late grant/SLA payments, poor grant administration by funders'. Another diocese pointed out: 'previous experience of poor cash flow and uncertain funding led us to withdraw from this form of "contract" work in 2001'.

3.1.2 Human Resources
Naturally a capacity assessment requires a judgement about financial resources, and also about the human skills, talent and creativity that are available to the Church. We looked at each Diocesan Church House, normally the administrative headquarters

of a diocese. The 28 dioceses that returned our questionnaire employed a total of 994 people in Church Houses or headquarters, with most dioceses employing between 20 and 40 people (Chart 4). The majority of these employees are paid lay people, although 24 dioceses employ ordained ministers as well. One diocese employs 16 priests! Volunteers comprise a very small proportion overall of Church House employees.

Chart 4. Number of Staff in Surveyed dioceses

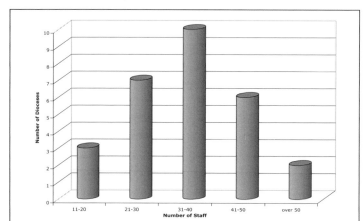

We asked dioceses to indicate how many of their staff held accounting/administrative qualifications or experience. Of the 27 dioceses who answered the question, 6 employed over 10 people with such qualifications or experience (Chart 5). In sum, 217 of the 994 total employees (22%) had these qualifications, which, arguably, is higher than the norm for regional organisations in the third sector.

Chart 5. Staff with Accounting / Administrative Backgrounds

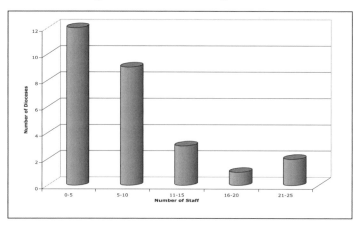

When asked how many employees have professional or management qualifications and/or experiences, the trend continues. Of the 19 dioceses answering this question, 4 reported employing over 10 individuals with these qualifications (Chart 6). Of the 812 employees listed by the 19 finance officers, 147 were reported as possessing professional or management qualifications (18%).

Chart 6. Staff with Professional/Management Qualifications

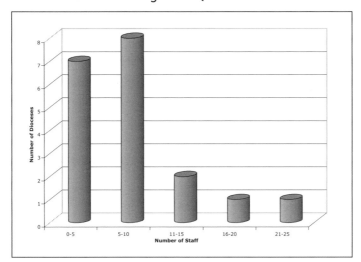

Out of the 11 dioceses that currently receive state funding for welfare provision, 8 reported having up to 10 employees with accounting/administrative background and 5 reported having up to 10 members of staff with professional/management qualifications.

The data also suggest that those dioceses that currently do not receive state funding for social welfare services have staff who might already be equipped to engage in contracting and tendering. If dioceses with minimal staff possessing these qualifications have been able to receive funding from the state, then in principle the remaining dioceses have such potential too, given their stronger financial and skills capacity.

Indeed, we asked how many of the in–house staff had experience of developing or negotiating service level agreements (SLA) in either the public or private sector. 8 of the 20 responding dioceses reported 3 or more employees with such experience (Chart 7). Again the numbers were not insignificant. At the same time, only 3 out of 16 believed there was someone else in the diocese whom they could call on for such help, so communication seems to be a key area for development if dioceses want to explore new activities of any kind.

Chart 7. Staff with Experience of Service Level Agreements (SLA)

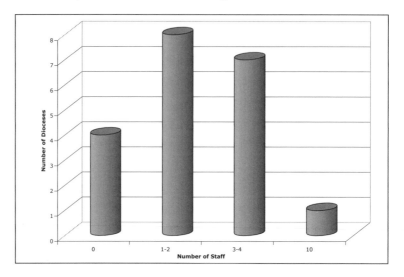

Separately we asked how many staff had experience of contracting with statutory bodies. 12 dioceses reported having no staff meeting this criterion, while the remaining 16 reported having at least one with experience of contracts (Chart 8). The three dioceses reporting between 4-10 employees already are engaged in providing social welfare services on state funding, and only two out of 11 contracting dioceses have no such member of staff. Again the number was not proportionately small.

Chart 8. Staff with Experience of Contracting with Statutory Bodies

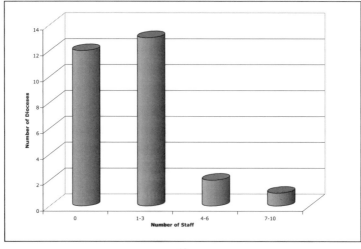

Dioceses were asked to specify further how many staff had experience of contracting at different levels of funding. At the lowest levels (up to £250,000), many dioceses (20) have several staff with experience of contracts. As the contracts become larger (£500,000, over £1 million), the number of staff with experience tends to decrease, but still is not proportionately small (Charts 9-11).

Charts 9-11. Staff with Experience at Different Levels of Contracts

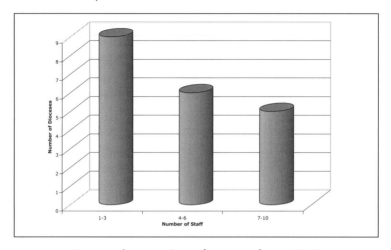

How many have experience of contracts of up to £250K?

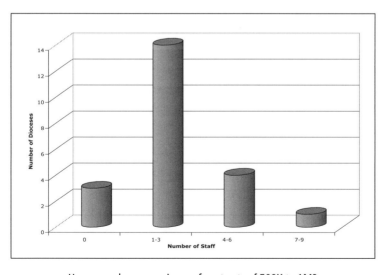

How many have experience of contracts of 500K to 1M?

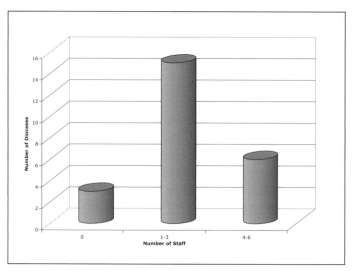

How many have experience of contracts of over £1M?

When these figures are cross-tabulated with the question: does the diocese provide social welfare services on state funding, the results are rather interesting. The majority of dioceses reporting the highest numbers of staff with contract experience have already accepted state funding for social welfare services.

At the same time, most of the dioceses employing 1-3 members of staff with experience of negotiating contracts in all three ranges of funding are not currently receiving state funding. The fact remains that dioceses in the Church of England have a great deal of untapped experience at their disposal.

3.1.3 Surveys, in Sum
Even excluding their important role in the provision of Academies or maintained, voluntary aided and voluntary controlled schools, Anglican dioceses have considerable levels of skill, assets and other resources at their disposal. With the right kind of infrastructure funding this, in theory, could make them a potential partner in the development of fresh service provision and social innovation initiatives.

At present, however, the nature of contracts secured does not seem to have been an easy journey for most dioceses. The skills and resources of contracting dioceses are not so different from non-contracting ones. All are facing potentially more demanding management problems.

3.2 Cathedrals: Regional Power Houses in Local Communities

To get a broader view of the Church's current and potential contribution to civil society and the common good, we examined the role of English cathedrals alongside our diocesan enquiry. We focused on these (mostly) ancient institutions partly because we were interested in the reported increase in cathedral congregations and partly because the Church's directories showed that significant numbers of staff (many of whom were senior clergy) were concentrated in cathedral precincts. In the course of our research we found a significant number of cathedrals that had experienced great renewal after 'reinventing' themselves as both visitor attractions and as spiritual centres.

Those who work in cathedrals often claim that, 'cathedrals in England are first and foremost places of worship'. This rather clichéd assertion will not convey the viewpoint articulated during several interviews: '*everything* that goes on in and around a cathedral is a form of worship', especially because 'cathedrals inherit the traditions of hospitality which were present in their founding communities'. Additionally, if one follows the 'performance figures' and assumes that those who attend cathedrals outside formal worship are not there to pray, it may be quite easy to underestimate the overall impact of these historic centres of community. One social entrepreneur went so far as to argue that cathedrals deliver 'a "quadruple bottom line" of social, economic, civic and mission value'. In his view it was no wonder that cathedrals 'are experiencing an increase in regular worshipping attendance, school student participation numbers and community and music outreach'.

From the heart of the government one junior minister spoke about how moving from the inner city to take up a cathedral school scholarship changed his life. 'I went from one strong community to another, and I have come back to the community I represent knowing that youth work, pioneering homelessness action and community participation would not be the same without the contribution of the churches'. If the Church of England is going to consider new activities, cathedrals seem to be crucial hubs that might encourage 'clustering' of potentially positive social and economic impacts.

In 2007 the Association of Leading Visitor Attractions named 2 Anglican cathedrals in the top 20 places visited in England: St Paul's (1,623,881) and Canterbury (1,068,244).[93] Indeed, economically cathedrals contribute both directly and indirectly to the community through employment and the spending habits of visitors. They serve as spaces to educate young and old about history, art, architecture, music and religion. Several provide outreach and social provisions to

---

93 http://www.alva.org.uk/visitor_statistics/

the marginalised in their environs. Many offer their space to other organisations to use for concerts, meetings, conferences and other events. With an estimated 8.8 million visitors in 2003, cathedrals are clearly important tourist destinations and economy boosters.[94]

Contributions to the local community from cathedral visitors were estimated in 2003 to be approximately £91 million (with total procurement this increases to £150m), which supports about 2600 FTE jobs throughout England. Furthermore, cathedrals spent at least £21 million on wages and salaries in 2003, directly employing 1885 FTE workers. The six largest cathedrals (Canterbury, Durham, St Paul's, Salisbury, Winchester and York) employed an average of 114 FTE employees who worked in bookshops, educational centres, and cafes or restaurants. Based on the total procurement figures from these dioceses, an additional 170 FTE jobs were created in local economies in the see cities. In sum, Anglican cathedrals in England provided directly and indirectly for 5450 FTE jobs, roughly the number of people who are currently employed by Ryanair,[95] the largest budget airline in Europe in terms of passengers, and twice the number employed by Avon Cosmetics, one of the top three beauty brands in the UK.[96]

Most cathedrals have worked to develop educational programmes linked to the National Curriculum and Agreed Syllabuses so as to attract school groups to visit. The independent research and consulting firm, ECOTEC, reported[97] that in 2003 over 362,000 people had benefited from educational visits at 35 cathedrals, a figure considered to be underestimated because some schools do not take advantage of the cathedral's education staff. According to the Church Heritage Forum's report, *Building Faith in Our Future*,[98] 39,749 students visited the cathedrals of Bristol, Exeter, Gloucester, Salisbury, Truro and Wells in 2002, while another 18,000 school children utilise Winchester Cathedral's educational programme each year.

At York Minster students can learn about 'Romans, Anglo Saxons and Vikings in Britain', while at Coventry Cathedral they can participate in a programme about the

---

94 ECOTEC Research and Consulting Ltd for English Heritage and the Association of English Cathedrals (2004) *The Economic and Social Impacts of Cathedrals in England.*

95 Based on figures presented in Ryanair's 2006 Annual Report and in the About Us section of Ryanair's website: http://www.ryanair.com

96 Information provided by Midland HR in 'Avon Cosmetics sees the beauty in Trent from Midland HR'.

97 ECOTEC op cit.

98 Church Heritage Forum (2004) *Building Faith in Our Future*, Church House Publishing.

Blitz or focus on 'Conflict, Peace and Resolution'. At Canterbury, students in years 2-6 learn about the story of Thomas Becket through an interactive process. History, art, religion and architecture come to life through educational opportunities provided by the majority of the Anglican cathedrals. Furthermore, several cathedrals also provide adult learning facilities for the wider community. In Wakefield, the cathedral's Westmorland Centre works 'to advance the education of the general public by the provision of an education centre and learning resource' and 'to provide a safe and secure environment for the development of individual skills and the future potential of young people by means of inclusion and empowerment' through free courses in ICT, literacy and numeracy.[99]

As we have indicated, moves are underway to rejuvenate the English choral tradition by meshing the government's Academies programme with the renewal of cathedrals as centres of culture. In Bristol the private sector cathedral school was brought into the state sector and has experienced a leap in applications. It is hoped that this success will be replicated in other cathedrals. Indeed, thanks to the work of Frank Field MP and Mgr James Cronin there is a good chance that this idea will be taken on by other Christian churches as well. Robert Key MP also expressed powerful enthusiasm for the potential of cathedrals after his positive experiences with the dean of Salisbury Cathedral and clergy and lay volunteers from the wider diocese.

Several cathedrals preserve major English historical documents and artefacts and this heritage and scholarship role is seen as a key function of their religious service. One of the few existing copies of the Magna Carta is housed at Lincoln Cathedral. Canterbury's Cathedral Library and Archives contains over 1300 years of history and knowledge in the form of books and manuscripts, including several key documents in English history.

Because of their prominent position within communities, cathedrals can serve as centres of social action too. This can help to promote community cohesion and/or participation. For example, in Blackburn a post has been created to support the growing numbers of refugees and asylum seekers (Appendix C), while the Manchester Cathedral serves the homeless through the Booth Centre. Based at the cathedral, this drop-in centre opened in 1995 to provide the homeless with empowering support to resolve their problems and with activities geared to tap into their creative side.

---

99 www.wakefieldcathedral.org.uk/outreach.html

At Sheffield Cathedral, the Cathedral Archer Project (CAP)[100] provides the homeless with free breakfast, an inexpensive lunch, basic education (life skills, numeracy, literacy), a nurse and a dentist who come once a month, and food parcels for those who are seeking asylum. Through partnerships with other organisations, each individual who comes to CAP can meet with those groups who can assist them the most in trying to change their lives. In 2003, Sheffield Cathedral was recognised nationally for this work with the homeless, winning the Queen's Award for Voluntary Service. In order to provide better facilities for CAP and to expand the services currently being offered, the Cathedral opened the £4 million Community Resources Centre in March 2007.

Coventry Cathedral houses the International Centre for Reconciliation (ICR), established in 1940 as one of the first religious-based centres for reconciliation. What began with a focus on reconciliation with Britain's enemies has since spread into conflict resolution work throughout the world. The ICR today 'is committed to reconciliation in various situations of violent conflict, some related to religious dispute and others fuelled by different factors' and 'coordinates the Community of the Cross of Nails, an international network of over 150 organisations in 60 countries committed to reconciliation'.[101] The work of the ICR promotes peace-making and cross-community dialogue, both at home and abroad.

Based on ECOTEC's survey results,[102] all cathedrals were used 3-5 times per week for various events. The most utilised seem to be the smaller 'parish church' cathedrals from the youngest dioceses, as they are often the community's largest venue. The breadth of cultural events and activities is staggering, ranging from chamber concerts in Bradford to stand-up comedy in Truro (not to mention their restaurant and coffee shop). In Lincoln the 13th-century subdeanery has been converted into the Cathedral Centre, which is open to visitors and locals, and contains a number of rooms, which can be rented by groups and businesses. Canterbury's Cathedral Lodge and International Study Centre provide accommodation and meeting spaces for conferences and for business groups meeting in Kent. The cathedral in Truro was even used in 2005 to provide space for a Madrasah (school) for the small local Muslim population, helping to build inter-religious dialogue and community cohesion.

Summarising Capacity
Cathedrals are concentrations of talent and resources that may be crucial if the Church in some regions were to consider enhancing either its advocacy or service delivery.

---

100 For more information on the Cathedral Archer Project and other activities at Sheffield Cathedral, visit http://www.sheffield-cathedral.co.uk/.

101 http://www.coventrycathedral.org.uk/bkground.html

102 Ecotec op cit.

In terms of experience, capacity and capability, they stand head and shoulders above the government's new FaithAction network - which in some regions consists of a lone freelance consultant - or even of many Councils for Voluntary Service. The Archdeacon of Craven reflected, 'one could even think of these bodies (cathedrals) as community foundations because that would certainly be the ethos in which so many of them were founded'. A former civil servant at DfID further developed this idea, arguing that 'Government could be well advised on the home front to develop trust, a risk culture, new energy by allocating budgets to cathedrals and dioceses to invest openly in local civic initiative across the board'.

3.3 Bishops

Within most Anglican traditions, bishops are said to have important symbolic, unifying and/or leadership roles within their dioceses. Many of our respondents also recognised the likelihood that media enquiries would, in the first place, be often channelled to bishops' offices.

We surveyed Anglican bishops to ask them what their 'civic contribution' was beyond the life of their liturgical responsibilities, which they still judged to be a major part of their ministry. We did not include contribution bishops make to the work of the House of Lords.

More than half of all 106 bishops responded to our survey, including the offices of the Archbishops of Canterbury and York. We complemented this data with an examination of diocesan websites and with feedback from a workshop in Derbyshire attended by approximately forty bishops. At the same residential event a plenary debate was held for bishops from England, Wales, Ireland and Scotland, including contributions from the Bishops of Worcester, Canterbury, York and Liverpool. Overall we found the bishops to be socially concerned and highly active in the civic arena, with their fundamental direction of work pointing outwards to the full realm of society.

The picture that emerged was of bishops having a strong sense of responsibility and engagement with the geographical *space and place* represented by their diocesan boundaries and *not simply* focused on their congregations. In some cases this geographical space was co-terminous with a particular county administrative area, while in others the remit was broader.

Activities of the Bishops in the Church of England

- 38 were on the governing body of a university, school, further education college or specialist college for people with learning disabilities;

- 11 were involved in the local city or county community foundation or had ring-fenced charitable giving plans with similar community purposes:
    - Two assisted in the launch of the community foundation;
    - Several are office holders in the community foundation either as Chair, Vice Chair or board member;
    - One established a 'Bishop's Fund' to provide multiple small grants of £250 or less to community groups of all backgrounds where this would make a big difference to their work;
    - One established a Bishop's Foundation, which worked in partnership with the community foundation;
- 8 were on a national state or voluntary sector working party, commission or body, including the National Police Improvement Authority, the NHS Working Party on End of Life Care, the Social Justice Commission of the Labour Party, the Stephen Lawrence Enquiry, the Carnegie Enquiry into the Rural Voluntary Sector, and the Third Sector Review;
- 18 were Chair or board member of a local statutory or multi-agency body concerned with unemployment, social and economic regeneration, including New Deal, local strategic partnerships (LSPs), the county community education committee, a City Centre management team, and a rural county voluntary sector consortium;
- 5 were involved in cultural or community sport projects linked to regeneration or the renewal of buildings other than churches;
- 51 were involved in fundraising appeals and activities for local community causes such as think tanks and hospices, training bodies and children's bodies, older peoples agencies and health charities, overseas aid and third world solidarity;
    - The Archbishop of Canterbury has lent his name as patron or president to some 300 organisations!
- Several were engaged in national charities focused on children, housing and education;
    - One had been on the board of the National Housing Federation and now chaired its Charitable Trust nationally;
    - Another chairs the national charity Mental Health Matters;
    - The Bishop of Leicester is chair of the £50 million per annum

> Children's Society, which nationally has extensive partnerships and contracting agreements with local state bodies.;

- 26 structured and/or planned meetings, liaised with Chief Constables, City and County Chief Executives, and leading health authority and primary care trust figures, and had good links with local councillors and Members of Parliament;

  o Several convened a regular civic leaders' breakfast involving those from across public, private and/or voluntary sectors.

Several of the bishops reported that their engagements in civil society were long-standing, in many cases starting before their appointment to episcopal orders. New areas of civil society participation, such as regeneration or community development, often are handed over to archdeacons when the bishop cannot take on any more work.

In the future it will be important to develop research into the civic contribution of deans, archdeacons, and cathedral canons, as well as clergy at the local level, if the variety of Anglican engagement in English society is to be fully understood.

3.4 Below the Radar: Congregations and Volunteering

Using the DCLG's Citizenship Survey, the NCVO has discounted the idea that there is any positive correlation between *religious conviction* and habits of volunteering or wider civic action. However, a significant number of studies show a positive correlation between *church attendance* and civic habits, while others, at least thus far, show a positive correlation between religious conviction[103] and the ability to adjust to the ageing process with positive mental health.[104] Some US studies go further, revealing a relationship between the form of Christian theological or denominational affiliation and the nature and extent of civic engagement, suggesting that religious ideas do have public consequences for both personal and institutional practice.[105]

We recognise that the debate between 'believing' and 'belonging' remains unresolved, but it was not within the scope of our present brief to address the topic fully. Regardless

---

103 R. Wuthnow (1999) 'Mobilising Civic Engagement: The Changing Impact of Religious Involvement' in T. Skocpol & M. Fiorina (eds) *Civic Engagement in American Democracy* Brookings Institution/ Sage.

104 P.G. Coleman (2006) *Spirituality, Health and Ageing*. David Hoberman Lecture. Institute of Gerontology, King's College, London.

105 See the work of Professor Dean Hoge, Catholic University of America. http://sociology.cua.edu/faculty.Hoge.cfm

of the true motivational forces that move Christians to participate in civil society, we have discovered a wealth of activities occurring on the congregational and other local levels of the Church. While our main analysis has been on the 'bigger picture' of dioceses, we believe it is nonetheless important to note aspects of this rooted local action.

In surveying published and unpublished research we have recorded a veritable empire of civil society founded, funded, sustained and maintained by Christian congregations, churches and believers. These initiatives endure alongside, through, and sometimes despite Church and/or government structures.

The initiatives we discovered, as the myriad case studies in Appendix C demonstrate, nestle at the heart of congregational life, arise from a cluster of churches or faith groups, occur at the diocesan or national level or even survive regionally. These initiatives may also mobilise extensive Anglican community assets to build community and participation.

In every government region we have found congregations, clergy and volunteers running post offices and cafes, doctors' surgeries and asylum rights centres, homeless outreach and bereavement counselling, job creation and economic regeneration programmes, eco initiatives and youth clubs, peace networks and third world solidarity groups. Many of these examples would not be captured in the Charity Commission's statistics given their decision to define 'relieving poverty' as distinct from 'advancement of religion', for they are organised directly from the heart of congregations without judgement or conditions attached. The majority of these initiatives are run on voluntary activity, which we will focus on below. However, when appropriate we have made reference to paid work as well.

In the Diocese of Southwell and Nottingham statistics were collected in 2005 as part of archdeacons' visits to local parishes.[106] An excess of 1250 volunteers organised work with 0-10 year olds, and 85 different churches offered support to toddlers and their carers with 2,550 people attending these groups each month. In 80 churches, clubs were being provided for more than 1,343 elderly people each month. Some 78 church based youth clubs were active with 1037 young people attending each month, while 2336 children and young people attended holiday clubs and schemes run by churches in the last year.

---

106 Information provided by R. Payne at Church House, Westminster. We acknowledge Payne's unpublished case studies of Anglican civic involvement, some of which we draw upon in this report.

103 churches had some form of practical help scheme for those who are housebound. 26 worked with the homeless, and 13 offered practical support to refugees and asylum seekers (i.e. food, clothing, information, gathering evidence in support of appeals). 48 churches provided support and counselling for ex-offenders and for those with problem patterns of drug and alcohol use.

A Derbyshire study painted a similar picture.[107] The 277 returned questionnaires showed volunteers in 190 churches giving 85,000 hours of their time, plus an additional 80,000 hours contributed by individuals (deemed by that study to be an underestimation). 25% of the volunteers for Church-run activities were from the local community, suggesting not only that church members become engaged by the work done by faith communities, but also that such action can act as a catalyst for the wider community.

In 2002 respondents to a survey across the 33 London boroughs named more than 2,000 projects aimed at the local community with roughly 13,500 volunteers.[108] If the data accurately serves as a predictor for the large number of faith communities that did not respond, the figures are likely closer to 7,000 projects and 45,000 volunteers.

In the East of England an estimated 49,000 volunteers support 5000+ social and community projects. The valuation of the time they give is over £30 million, meaning about £582,000 each week.[109] The North West has 45,667 volunteers belonging to different faiths who give over 8 million hours of time (4815 FTE jobs) each year and generate between £60.6 and £65.6 million.[110] In the South West, at least 10,000 volunteers serve in different capacities, with estimates ranging to about 50,000 in the entire region.[111]

Returning to more specifically Christian action, a report from the Churches Commission for Yorkshire and Humberside painted a very active picture. Entitled *Angels and Advocates: Church Social Action in Yorkshire and the Humber*, it suggested that the 4500 churches in the region engage in some 6500 social action projects.

---

107 Derby Diocesan Council for Social Responsibility (2006) *Faith in Derbyshire: Working Towards a Better Derbyshire, faith-based contribution.*

108 L. Anderson, T. Drummond, E. Simon & M. Williams (2004) *Regenerating London: Faith Communities and Social Action*, Greater London Enterprises & London Churches Group.

109 East of England Faiths Council and the University of Cambridge (2005) *Faith in the East of England.*

110 Churches Officer for the Northwest and the Regional Intelligence Unit (2003) *Faith in the North West.*

111 Faithnetsouthwest. *Faith in Action in the South West.*

Over 50,000 churchgoers are regularly involved in church-based or -supported social action, and a similar number engage in social action not organised by the churches. Roughly 3,000 staff work on church projects with over 150,000 people benefiting regularly. The report estimated the economic value of church social action to the region as approximately £60 million a year.

'The Church is dependent upon a very hard-working group of volunteers', claimed one recent report.[112] Contrary to what might be assumed, the success of projects depends more on volunteers than on funding. 36% of respondents in the East of England indicated that projects had failed due to a lack of volunteers, while only 26% said it was because of a lack of money.[113] When churches in Derbyshire were asked, 'What was/would be needed to maintain or develop similar activities or services?' the largest number (25) responded with 'recruit and support volunteers'.[114]

The Commission on the Future of Volunteering has noted many benefits of volunteering, both for the community and for the volunteer. This is true of faith-based, inspired, motivated and trained volunteers. One study spoke of the importance of volunteering linked to churches for those who are retired or perhaps are too ill to work full-time, as they can put the skills honed over the years to good use.

Furthermore, citizens gain new skills and capacities through volunteering mobilised by their church community. Skill acquisition can occur either through formalised training or through experience, and may be 'a way back into the labour market for economically vulnerable individuals',[115] especially those from refugee and asylum networks whose link with churches is reportedly increasing.

The Diocese of Birmingham is exemplar when it comes to the engagement of excluded groups. Despite having some of the poorest congregations in the country - at an average income of £12,000 per annum, below even the Charity Commission's new monitoring threshold of £100,000 for excepted charities such as parishes - and despite covering some of the most diverse neighbourhoods in the UK, the diocese maintains 57 community projects that provide activities for 38,000 visitors each week.[116]

---

112 Diocese of Oxford (2004) *Faith in Culture: A Faith Contribution to Cultural Strategies.*
113 *Faith in the East of England* op cit.
114 *Faith in Derbyshire* op cit.
115 Regional Action West Midlands (2006) *Believing in the Region: A baseline study of aith bodies across the West Midlands.*
116 From website of Diocese of Birmingham, December 2007 www.birmingham.anglican.org

More than 900 volunteers, 179 part-time staff and 172 full-time staff work for these church-based community projects. These initiatives include day care centres for the elderly, community centres, holiday schemes and after school clubs, a SureStart project, a healthy eating café, a drop-in centre, charity shops, an IT skills training centre, an economic regeneration centre providing advice on jobs, parent and toddler groups, a housing association focusing on homeless young people, a support network for those with disabilities, a centre for people with dementia, chronic conditions support groups, and an academic centre specialising in researching ageing, social policy and the community. In passing we ought also to mention that each week an average of 19,100 people, including 3500 children and young people, worship in an Anglican church in the Birmingham Diocese. All of this activity both on Sunday and on the other days of the week comprises a 'rich outpouring of what it means to be ourselves'.

In 2004 the Thomas Low Partnership published a report noting that Christian congregations in the city of Bradford employed 150 people in social action initiatives. Based on the then minimum wage of £4.85 an hour, this work was valued at over £1.3m per year. Over 2,100 Christians were involved in delivering church-based social action on a voluntary basis. With each volunteer serving an average of 4 hours per week, the accumulated effort totalled 430,000 volunteer hours per annum![117]

These patterns are not confined to the North, East and the Midlands, important though they are in those regions. The Dioceses of Winchester, Guildford and Portsmouth collaborate to manage a neighbourhood care group network funded on a service level agreement by Hampshire County Council and involving 3000 volunteers from every social class and religious background. The social responsibility officers for the three dioceses are among the most entrepreneurial in the UK.[118]

A 2004 survey in Hastings (Chichester Diocese) commissioned by Hastings Voluntary Action and carried out by Churches Together in Hastings and St Leonards discovered:[119]

- 8 out of 10 churches provide services that are of benefit to people who are not part of their congregations;
- 1,200 hours of voluntary work were given to the community each week, the equivalent of 22 full-time staff working 52 weeks a year;

---

117 Shaftesbury Society (2006) *Challenging Church.*
118 Interviews with Nick Ralph, Chris Rich and other regional clergy in the SEEDA area.
119 R. Payne op cit.

- Churches on average each ran two community projects, and much of their work – often done ecumenically – is focused on hard-to-reach groups such as excluded young people, drug addicts, refugees, and asylum seekers.

Pam Brown, then Mayor of Hastings, said in February 2005, 'the Church is a significant provider of volunteers and its work has greatly impacted on the community of Hastings and St Leonards'.

Despite the overwhelmingly positive view of volunteering portrayed in these regional studies, there are also pockets of concern that will need to be addressed if the Church and other faith communities are going to sustain – or expand upon- their activities. First, the advanced age of volunteers in some (but not all) churches and areas brings into question the sustainability of current projects and/or the birth of new ones without the employment of paid staff. For example, a questionnaire survey conducted in the Dioceses of Durham and Newcastle found that the average age of volunteers in certain churches was over 80![120]

Second, while the regional studies overwhelmingly point to the increase in community capacity that arises from extensive church and wider faith-based volunteering, several draw attention to the difficulties that inexperienced volunteers can have when charged with responsibility for complex application forms, funding bids and legislative compliance. Increasing regulation and personal risk were often reported to us as reasons why volunteers were likely not to come forward. Despite NCVO's insistence that Church groups ought to 'sign up to mainstream networks,' church groups rarely turn to local councils or NCVO for information and support. Many prefer to look to the diocese or to their local representative of Churches Together in England. Voluntary and social action in the Church of England would, it seems, be greatly enhanced by building up its own networks of facilitation and support.

3.5 Community Assets and Buildings

The full range of parish-owned halls and other assets was outside the scope of our study. However, nationally there is evidence to suggest that they are potentially a significant community resource – albeit with limitations of planning and finance.

For example, in the West Midlands, 88% of faith communities granted other groups access to their buildings for conferences, Alcoholics Anonymous meetings, police public meetings, theatre and music.[121] A study in the East of England found that 74%

---

120 F. Clarke *Coalfields Regeneration in North East England: The Contribution of Faith Communities.*
121 *Believing in the Region* op cit.

of faith communities do likewise, providing community rooms and meeting space to other groups, especially young people's organisations like the Scouts.[122] 1385 places of worship in the North West rented out rooms for community use,[123] while *Faith in the Southwest* reports that 549 faith communities (65% of those polled) have buildings used for community purposes, with 8% hosting ten or more activities.

3.6 Evidence from Home & Afield: The Spirit Of Social Innovation[124]

As previously demonstrated, the Church has historically acted as a source of social innovation by identifying unmet needs and launching new organisations and policy ideas to respond to them. Often Church ideas have then been appropriated by the state when deemed successful. For example, at the 2008 Labour Party Spring Conference, Rt Hon Ed Miliband MP claimed the successes of the 'Living Wage' campaign as a victory for Labour, even though it had been wholly invented and driven by faith-based energy until the trade unions belatedly joined its cause.

Nevertheless, during the course of our research it has become increasingly clear to us that neither Government nor the Church has been particularly effective at drawing together insights across departments or in learning from Christian bodies internationally. Since Christian churches have founded and run more schools, orphanages, hospitals and community projects than the UK state, this seems an area where new work naturally could be undertaken.

3.6.1 A New Anglican Philanthropy?

Such new work clearly needs funding, and so we turn briefly to the question of philanthropy within the Church of England. The promulgation of *Faith in the City* led to the creation of the Church Urban Fund (CUF), which was to target charitable resources on poor neighbourhoods. We were told frequently that the climate that enabled successful fundraising for the Church Urban Fund in the eighties and early nineties 'no longer exists', because donors no longer want to support an intermediary body that does not allow them to partner with the community organisations to whom they are giving funding. Donors also now prefer to add value to their 'investment'

---

122 *Faith in the East of England* op cit.

123 *Faith in the Northwest* op cit.

124 For a view of social innovation that is policy led, see G. Mulgan et al (2006) *Social Silicon Valleys*, Young Foundation. For a faith-based critique and advocacy of a more human and passionate approach, see A. Elliott (2006) 'The Spirit Of Social Innovation,' a lecture for the International Futures Forum at the Scottish Parliament (www.internationalfuturesforum.com/iff-publications. php). Elliott is the former Moderator of the Church of Scotland and based currently at New College, Edinburgh University.

in a hands-on way by donating time, skills and networks. Yet Jan Ainsworth at the Board of Education informed us that tens of millions of new philanthropic funds had been raised for the Church's Academies programme in a very short time. Ainsworth and others had also established a network of social enterprises to support the Academies programme by using joint purchasing power, training insights and shared management skills to help new Academies get started.

The time available for the present project has not permitted a full exploration of the potentialities of what might be called 'a new Anglican philanthropy' in the social sphere. The experience at the Board of Education seemed to indicate that the 'right ask, fresh ideas, and focus would lead to the right result', thereby leading to the release of new gifts.

Three consultancies – who knew we were not offering business – confirmed this insight, as did a leading third sector provider of advice to high net worth donors. One went so far as to recommend that 'A Lambeth Social Innovation Fund' to back experimental, risk taking, and micro-finance style activities in poor communities would be a unique contribution the Church could make to developing 'fresh expressions of social action'.

Indeed, we were told that there may be opportunities to create new philanthropic vehicles or reinvent old ones. One model to learn from will be the 'Lambeth Partners'' network of regular donors to key Anglican causes established by Archbishop George Carey. Other insights could be gleaned from learning from other donor networks established by some banks and internationally. The bishops might also wish to turn to work being done in the United States by Robert Wuthnow and others for insights into how such faith philanthropy might enhance the life of the Church and what shape it might take.

Reflection on new philanthropic resources is not simply a traditional call to new fundraising, but rather the backdrop to constructive thinking about what may be possible as a fresh Anglican response in our times.

3.6.2 Learning from across the Anglican Communion

The Anglican Communion in recent years has received much attention because of doctrinal and theological disputes. Sadly, in our view, not enough acknowledgement has been made of the sharing of best practice that has begun on overseas development, university education and microfinance either officially via the Communion or in new projects arising from the last Lambeth Conference. Likewise, the important work of the Church Mission Society (CMS) and USPG: Anglicans in World Mission has been overlooked in their particular spheres of influence.

There would seem to be immense scope for the sharing of insights on many issues, including the role of the Church in welfare provision, especially because many societies within the Communion are facing state restructuring, the impact of the new public management and the perennial challenges of funding and changes in the nature of need.

In South Africa pioneering self-funding models of social and health care in the third sector have been founded. Innovative Church responses to community participation are to be found in the US and Canada, while in New Zealand and Australia advanced work and experience of welfare reform provides valuable insights.

If the government scours the world looking for fresh policy models, why should the Church not draw upon its own rich international memory and experience?

As examples of some models of interest arising from within the Anglican Communion, we turn now to the work of Anglicare and the Brotherhood of St Laurence, both based in Australia, and the Hong Kong Sheng Kung Hui Welfare Council. In doing so, we drew heavily on insights taken from Bishop Stephen Lowe's study tour to Australia and Asia as a complementary strand of our own study.

Anglicare Victoria

Anglicare is part of a nationwide network of Anglican social services, and is the state's largest non-governmental child and family welfare agency. Founded in July 1997 following the amalgamation of three existing child and welfare agencies with a combined history of more than 260 years, it currently has 627 paid staff and 1600 volunteers enabling it to run 100 different programmes across forty locations. In total, Anglicare provides support to more than 50,000 of the most disadvantaged and vulnerable people in the state. It is the largest provider of foster care in Victoria, helping some 3,000 children every year. By voluntary sector standards in Australia, Anglicare is a major actor.

It has a wide ranging remit: emergency relief and crisis accommodation for vulnerable children, young people and families; food and material aid to low income families; family support; foster care; counselling for victims of abuse and neglect; support for dealing with substance abuse, problem gambling, sexual assault and domestic violence; parent education and youth mentoring programmes; care for families with a child with a disability; youth accommodation and support; training and skills assistance for the unemployed; juvenile justice mediation and prison chaplaincy services; and financial counselling for low income earner.

Anglicare Victoria articulates its mission in explicitly theological terms: 'the agency exists to create a more just society by expressing God's love through service, education and advocacy'. References to its living Christian roots feature extensively in its reports and other documentation. As 'an agency drawn from the Christian faith' it argues that the core challenge it faces is understanding the meaning of 'being human' in the 21st century – which it answers in terms of 'respecting the dignity and rights of all children and families and particularly the disadvantaged'. This straightforward 'mission' is matched with the seriousness with which Anglicare takes its advocacy responsibilities.

Its social policy and research unit seeks to build a realistic understanding of the issues its 'clients' face, as well as matching these to overarching trends in society. This information is then used to ensure that government policy relating to issues such as material deprivation, social exclusion, homelessness, disability and young people at risk is designed around the poorest communities themselves.

Among the topics covered in its policy submissions in 2007 were restorative justice, the changing face of welfare, affordable housing, the impact of financial hardship on parenting behaviour, and young people's engagement with school. Remarkably, this advocacy is achieved even though Anglicare Victoria receives around three-quarters of its total income of A$43m from state government, Commonwealth government and local government sources. Its prophetic voice has not been silenced simply because it receives funding from the state.

On the contrary, Anglicare's staff believes that its position as provider enhances its advocacy potential. The agency has been prepared to reject government invitations to tender or provide when it has been unhappy about the nature of the service it is being requested to deliver. In 2006, for example, Anglicare joined with other church-based charitable organisations in refusing to implement the Howard government's 'Welfare to Work' programme. This programme, among other things, compelled disabled people to look for jobs and contained measures to deny unemployment benefits to single parents and disabled people for eight weeks for breaching job search rules. In a public statement the CEO of Anglicare Victoria said that his organization existed to 'support people, teach them skills and offer them resources and guidance to engage with their community' not 'to "mop up" after failed government policy'. 'We will not be part of a programme that blames disabled people, the mentally ill and other marginalised groups for their lack of engagement and punishes them so severely', he proclaimed.

The Brotherhood of St Laurence

The Brotherhood of St Laurence (BSL) is another important Anglican welfare provider in Australia. Among the services it offers are job training and placement programmes, care for the elderly and people with disabilities, early childhood development programmes and support services for newly arrived refugees and migrants. One of its leading members of staff has been a pioneer of Australian social enterprise.

BSL summarises its vision as 'An Australia free of poverty' and its mission 'to deliver services, develop policy and support social change'. It is clear that its aspiration is to alleviate poverty as well as to prevent it, focusing on people who are most vulnerable at four important life-stages: the early years, the years from school to work and further education, the periods in and out of work, and retirement and ageing. This life span approach contrasts interestingly with a geographical focus of, for example, the Church Urban Fund and many trained in the post-*Faith in the City* era in the UK.

BSL runs a number of social and community enterprises, the latter having an important training component for its young employees. Each operates on firmly ethical lines, with one social enterprise specialising in recycled clothing and home goods. The Brotherhood also promotes a 'Community Enterprise Development Initiative', which works with disadvantaged communities across Victoria to develop community enterprises.

Around 40% of BSL's annual income of A$50m comes from Government funds and contracts, with 30% secured through trading social enterprises and 18% from fundraising. Its provision of elderly and community care accounts for 37% of its outgoings, with around 31% invested in its social enterprises, 13% in community services and 11% on its employment programmes.

BSL aspires to be a national voice on matters of poverty and disadvantage, speaking from its experience as a service deliverer and innovator. It believes that the remedy to poverty lies in 'integrating social and economic policy as a basis to strengthening the capacities of individuals and communities' and seeks to reflect this analysis in its work. BSL makes submissions to federal and state commissions of enquiry once or twice per month.

A key feature of BSL's work is the emphasis it places on evidence-based advocacy. Consequently it has proposed new social partnership models for state-civil society partnership and been an outspoken critic of the government's use of the Household, Income and Labour Dynamics in Australia (HILDA) survey, which concluded that poverty was a 'short experience' for those Australians who experienced it. BSL has also been influential in applying Amartya Sen's capability theories to analyses of poverty in Australia, and this has led it to advocate an idea of 'the social investment state' rather than a 'welfare state'.

Like Anglicare, BSL declined to participate in the previous government's scheme to get unemployed people back to work with a greater emphasis on 'sticks' than 'carrots'. When explaining its objection BSL drew on its Christian basis: 'We see Christ in the unemployed, and we will not be part of visiting injustice upon them. Our role is to overturn laws that unjustly treat the disadvantaged, not to administer them'.

Hong Kong Sheng Kung Hui Welfare Council

The Hong Kong Sheng Kung Hui (HKSKH) Council was set up in 1973 by the Hong Kong Anglican Church to be its 'welfare arm' with responsibility for the co-ordination, development and provision of a variety of social services. Now independent of the Church – though with a very strong Christian foundation – the Council is one of the most prominent social welfare organisations in the country, with over 1,800 employees and a budget in excess of HK$440million (£28m). Stating that its 'Christian vision' is 'to build a society of justice, peace, love and care and our mission… based on the concept of "Individual Caring and Overall Concern"' the Council currently provides an enormous range of services for children, families, elderly people, immigrants and unemployed people.

Building on two centuries of engagement by the Church in social provision, the Council prides itself on the quality of its services, noting in its literature the various awards it has won in areas such as safety, infection control and hygiene. It was the first organisation in the Hong Kong social welfare sector to implement 'Total Quality Management'. A word much used in its publicity is 'integrated', and in all the strands of its work it seeks to address the needs of the 'whole person' and enable them, whether young or old, to enjoy the best possible quality of life.

This 'integrated' approach is perhaps most clearly represented in one of its recent projects, the 'Providence Garden for Rehab'. Opened in 2006 in Teun Mun this is, as its name suggests, a rehabilitation complex, and is targeted at serving 1000 users. The service components include a long-stay care home, a 'half-way house', a hostel and day-care activity centre for severely mentally disabled people, a hostel for what are termed 'moderate mental handicapped' people, a vocational centre and a care and attention home for severely disabled people.

Apart from the sheer scale of its programme what is noteworthy about the HKSKH Council is its relationship with the Communist Government of China. More than 71% of its funding comes in the form of Department for Social Welfare subvention, and projects such as the Providence Garden for Rehab have only been possible because of statutory funding of this sort. The resources for this particular project were in fact only made available after a competitive bidding process among non-governmental organisations initiated by the Government, in which the HKSKH Council was successful. What might be considered remarkable about this is not simply the fact that the Council is a Christian organisation but that it so explicitly relates its work to its principles.

Its annual reports and other literature are punctuated with quotations from Scripture, prayers and extracts from the writings of theologians, and it states clearly on its website – which has as its soundtrack the tune of 'Make Me a Channel of Your Peace' - that the Prayer of St. Francis is the motto of the co-workers, also the song of the Council. 'The co-workers do not only sing the song but also put it into practice', the website affirms. Its crest is also deeply symbolic of its mission, and it proudly explains in its literature the significance of each aspect including the shield – signifying 'the defending of the Christian faith in the temporal world'; the crown - which symbolises the kingship of Christ' and the fact that 'Church works in the world in obedience to Christ'; the Bible; the crozier; and 'the colours' – red and white symbolizing 'the sacrifice and holiness of Christ' and blue 'the working class of China, for Christ was Himself a carpenter'.

Mainland European and Ecumenical Potential

It is not within our brief to assess the European social policy debate fully nor to advocate for or against 'Europeanisation'. It is important to acknowledge the impact of EU legislation, but is perhaps even more important in the present context to record the very significant role the Churches play in social welfare provision and anti-poverty advocacy right across the EU and its 'applicant' countries.[125]

The re-emergence of Euro-Diakonia as a pan-European umbrella body is an important development in the Protestant Churches because social welfare provision among Reformed Christian agencies tends to be strongest where the Roman Catholic federation, Caritas Europa, is weakest. As the Lisbon process drives the marketisation of welfare, it may become increasingly important for these two ecumenical networks

---

125 See Caritas Europa's forthcoming (2008) *The European Social Inclusion Process, Civil Society and the Caritas Contribution.*

to cooperate. This could mean assessing how the new social partnership council in Ireland, or the older one in Sweden, might improve policy co-ordination and communication with the third sector.[126] Or it could mean drawing upon insights from huge national grassroots surveys on poverty led by the Churches in France and Germany.

Perhaps as significantly, such a European outlook would also allow the Church in England to draw on the experience of faith-based think tanks in a number of countries. Among these could be CORI Justice in Dublin whose annual analysis of the government's 'budget day' has become a major policy and political event.[127] Lessons could also be learned from the Stockholm Network and its success in developing international networks of smaller research institutes to build mutual learning and capacity, often in the face of limited resources.[128]

In Austria and Kosovo the Churches and faith groups drive 'social action' weeks involving thousands of young people who give their time to good causes. In stark contrast, UK Prime Minister Gordon Brown has established a National Council on Social Action which does not include any faith representatives![129]

When looking at capacity as well as policy issues the Church will need to build on ground-breaking projects such as the Foundation for Church Leadership. This might lead to finding fresh and creative means to network the social policy, management and business departments of Anglican and other Christian founded universities.[130]

In any event the European dimension to policy was greatly under-appreciated by the majority of our respondents. It is an area where the Church of England could learn a great deal from wider Anglican networks and ecumenical partners.

---

126 Interview with Dr George Joseph (Stockholm). On both partnership councils the third sector as a whole is represented by leading figures from the Churches. In some EU countries Church based voices have been the only ones seeking to bring the needs of the labour mobile, migrants, refugees and asylum seekers to the policy debate at national and EU level. It is striking that reporting on this aspect of exclusion is now a requirement from the EC in its anti-poverty planning.

127 CORI works across the policy community at both regional and cabinet level and with trade unions and businesses under the directorship of Sean Healy and Brigid Reynolds. See also *Developing a Fairer Ireland* (2006) Cori Justice, Dublin.

128 See www.stockholm-network.org for more information.

129 In Austria innovative work around migrant health developed by Christian Churches was specifically mentioned as a 'best practice' example in the 2006 National Social Inclusion Strategy.

130 This may include developing strategies to encourage 'leadership from the edges'. See M. Grundy (2007) *What's New In Church Leadership?* SCM.

PART 4: MORALS, MANAGEMENT AND COMMISSIONING

In this section we turn to reflect more on 'contracts'. Although it was not possible to develop a full theology of 'public management' at this juncture, there are key questions of principle and morality at stake for Christians in how contracts are designed and devised at every level of government. Even if a diocese, cathedral or other Anglican body decides not to engage in 'contracting' or some other form of civic action, it will need to make this decision in prayer, rigorous thought and coherent planning. In this section we also describe a Christian 'civic value' matrix, which we believe can help in this process (and might form a strong complementary tool to the Faithworks Charter).

4.1 Price, Performance, and Unconditional Solidarity

The qualitative feedback from dioceses, cathedrals and various Church networks and groups consistently raised a major concern about the government's current commissioning regime, even while many expressed an enthusiasm to engage with it.

These reservations took two consistent forms. As mentioned earlier, we were told that despite the efforts of 'Best Value', Government policies had the effect of encouraging purchasing managers to drive the agenda solely on 'price and aggressive readings of performance criteria'. This effectively was driving some purchasers away from the third sector.

On the other hand, our respondents raised the inadequacy of a 'qualitative' side to contract criteria, which undermines the 'Christian idea of unconditional solidarity'. For most of our respondents it is the qualitative, non-financial aspects of voluntary sector engagement in the building of care and empowerment that are key motivators. And yet many felt that these critical attributes of care and empowerment were being ignored – or under appreciated – by purchasers.

The Church-based projects we met at the community level (amongst others) emphasised the multi-dimensional nature of the poverty that they encountered and the extent to which 'simplistic', departmentalised targets did not allow for flexible accompaniment to address profound personal challenges experienced by those the projects serve. For some projects this tendency was compounded by the government's strategic selection of particular forms of welfare recipients for especial attention at the expense of the most needy. Christian projects claimed that what made them unique was the 'value added' performance that they brought to multi-dimensional care, which relatively unsophisticated targets impeded. In this regard the government's commissioning agenda is failing, despite the efforts of the 'Best Value' regime to allow some flexibility beyond price.

One possible solution may be the development of more flexible modes of funding such as those we have heard about from mainland European Christian social service organisations. This might mean a sophisticated horizontal budgeting requirement between departments like in France, a variant of which is being proposed by the Conservatives, or special accompaniment centres as currently being piloted in Spain. Irrespective of which model is used, the current structure of incentives and performance criteria is fundamentally failing to provide an appropriate environment to sustain and develop innovative and effective work alongside the poorest in society.

Unlike some in the Church, we acknowledge that Government-funded activities must be 'measured' rather than funded unconditionally. The challenge remains to devise new matrices that can improve understanding of attributes (i.e. spiritual, caring) that are involved in the full range of social activities in the eyes of the Church. The Cabinet Office's first attempts to move in this direction are a positive development. We also recognise that the Treasury had given the matter some consideration in the past. If we are not to undermine the generosity and passion with which faith-based and other volunteers contribute to civil society, these efforts must be deepened and trialled right across Whitehall – not least in those departments and non-departmental bodies with a penchant for huge head contracts.

A challenge still lingers for the Church. As we suggest in our recommendations, instead of complaining about existing measurement regimes, the Christian churches could work to commission the development of a 'Christian Value' tool to help Church groups demonstrate the full range of contributions they are making. Such a tool would greatly strengthen Faithworks 'faith standard' and the DCLG's expressed intention to use the standard as the basis for future faith-based contracting relationships. It could also help dioceses looking at 'public benefit' for the first time.

Perhaps more profoundly, if the Church calls on the government to set aside more flexible funding pools, is it also prepared to set aside its own resources with similar attitudes to risk, qualitative impact and social renewal? If the Church could find donors without reservations or demands regarding accountability, they may become beacons for new forms of 'unconditional solidarity'.

4.2 Towards a New 'Prophetic' Challenge?

Throughout this study we have encountered a Church struggling, often successfully, with the needs, concerns and aspirations of those among whom it is placed. We repeatedly encountered a powerful ethos and 'call to service'. As one leading Christian social entrepreneur reminded us, the Christian gospel at its very heart is about 'the Word being made Flesh', the outworking of which can be very messy but can have a major impact. Great sacrifice can accompany such work as well, but it is the Church's willingness to face this possibility that, in its view, separates it from other 'social' and 'caring' bodies.

As one priest who had worked in Brixton during the 1981 riots declared, 'it was a privilege to break bread with the families of the houses… to walk those streets and feel the tension and to know that we were one of the meeting places that were helping to bring people together'. Another priest said, 'we do not offer a bland liberal neutrality but the hope of resurrection. Without walking in the midst of the life of those who are being crucified we cannot preach that hope'. Still another shared with us the price that sometimes was paid: 'it can be costly in personal terms that by taking seriously the place in which we are rooted, we take seriously sharing in the lives of those who live there. In the poorest neighbourhoods this can only mean feeling their pain too'.

Stories such as these, related in countless interviews and through shared case studies, led us to see that this is the dimension of the Church's work that self-defines it as a Church *qua* Church rather than just another simplistically categorised voluntary sector agent. A Christian Church exists primarily to preach the Kingdom wherever it can. This task is defined not by Government, but rather by Scripture, tradition and the Spirit.

The priest who had worked in Brixton remarked, 'the Church of England is at its best when it is blessing the table of the family in trouble, walking the streets during a riot or disturbance, being with people in the gutter - despite all the rhetoric which suggests the opposite'. The Kingdom offers, we were told, a compelling vision of communities predicated on justice, peace and love, but the challenge of 'earthing' such a vision comes afresh to the Church in every age and in every situation.

Based on our interviews the Church of England needs now to struggle towards a fresh prophetic strategy, which will need to be grounded as much in deeds, service delivery and evidence as in words, statements and preaching. It would seem that the Church could help to transform welfare debates by engaging in civic action and delivery in practice. It could build on this goal by calling for a 'commissioning' or 'contracting' regime that more closely reflects some key Christian principles outlined below.

We have previously noted the move towards the adoption of a 'faith standard' by the DCLG. Although the form that this standard finally takes will be subject to ongoing debate, its extension to other departments of state is judged to be important by many of our respondents.

Many interviewees spoke of the need for Government to move beyond the 'faith standard' to develop something akin to a 'commissioning standard', which sets out very clearly what third sector bodies can *expect of government* at the local, regional, and national level. This would not be another version of the 'compact' or a loose 'chartermark', but would be a strong guidance to a new approach.

Such a fresh vision could form a standard by which local Christian and other bodies assess local purchasing patterns and policies. It could also be the focus of a new call by Bishops and others to a stronger kind of social partnership in the UK.

4.3 Christian Principles for Commissioning

During the course of our research we noted that certain key themes or principles with respect to the contracting process and experience were consistently present among church-people, irrespective of their theological stance. We will develop these themes more fully in our subsequent work. We set them out in summary here in the hope that as wide a range of communities as possible may engage in debate about the Church's future direction. We also set them out so that current policy can be judged by standards more profound than simply 'what works'.

Sacrifice and Gift

Christianity is founded on a gift relationship, with Christians understanding the Incarnation on one level in terms of 'the Father' gifting 'the Son'. A core text from the Gospel of John encapsulates this, 'God so loved the world that he gave his only begotten Son' (Jn 3.16).

In response to this, Christians and churches have understood themselves to be called to 'service', both to people in their immediate location and to humanity more widely. Thus, as we were constantly reminded during the course of our research, churches will often want to act in their parish or locality in response to perceived needs without necessarily the 'incentive' of a commission from a governmental or other statutory body. This narrative of 'giving' of oneself to the community and seeking no 'return' is strong in the church circles we encountered and runs rather countercultural. As we have seen, the church often sees itself as an institution that exists primarily for the place where it is located and for the benefit of all of its parishioners.

When it comes to partnering with Government, those we surveyed made it clear that they will also always be looking for space to work that is 'beyond financial measurement' or that allows for unconditional moments of gift. Put another way, a Christian approach would require the flexibility to address underlying needs, isolation and challenges, even when this did not automatically address a Whitehall 'target'.

Covenant and Consistency

Whatever form its civic action and service provision takes, the Church sees itself as being in 'for the long-term', with the local priest often being the only 'professional' to stay in some neighbourhoods over a long period. Short-termism in contracting, therefore, not only has a disempowering effect but also can hinder the work being done at the grassroots.

Instead of contracts, we heard mention of partnerships or 'covenants'. In Scripture, covenants are binding commitments between two parties (usually God and an individual or nation), sealed with oaths, with duties and responsibilities that both parties must uphold. Covenants were by their very nature long-standing (see Gen 9.16 and Deut 29.14-15), thus powerfully underlining the commitment and consistency of the modern Church in service to the world.

Christians believe that a commitment to such consistency is healthy for the common good. Indeed, while such covenants are unlikely to be achievable in every policy sphere, we did hear from leading business academics that indicator and price driven purchasing is being phased out in parts of the private sector. In its place will be supply chain management, which is much more 'relational' in character. The principle of covenant would therefore seek to extend the basis for partnership beyond one to three-year funding rounds, so that civic capacity can be built consistently. Such a fundamental commitment would also likely enhance the scope for creativity and would enable churches, the wider sector and individuals to focus their energies on implementing long-term visions and on being innovative rather than on constantly chasing funding.

Voice and Prophecy

Christians place special importance on the role of 'prophecy'. Prophets of old called people 'to loose the bonds of injustice, to undo the thongs of the yoke, to let the oppressed go free, and break every yoke... to share your bread with the hungry, and bring the homeless poor into your house; when you see the naked, to cover them, and not to hide yourself from your own kin' (Is 58.6-7). Modern day prophecy continues the theme of serving as a 'voice' and advocate for the poorest and most marginalised in society (in Biblical terms, the widow, the orphan, the stranger).

Bearing this in mind, the Christians we have interviewed shared a conviction that for the Church to be 'authentic' in the commissioning relationship, it will require the freedom to use its research and service provision experience as a ground for giving a voice to those that current systems and policies are failing. The previously mentioned case study of Anglicare would be an excellent model of what would be required. Such an approach would also sit well with exhortations made by Cabinet Minister John Denham MP, calling upon faith groups to campaign against child poverty.

Subsidiarity and Empowerment

According to the Christian principle of subsidiarity, 'government should undertake only those initiatives which exceed the capacities of individuals or private groups acting independently. Government should not replace or destroy smaller communities and individual initiative.'[131] In brief, subsidiarity demands that initiatives and actions are undertaken at the lowest feasible level rather than the state running and controlling everything. Under such a principle, it is government's task to *assist* these smaller groups or organisations to 'contribute more effectively to social well-being'. This assistance would certainly, in the eyes of those with whom we spoke, come in the shape of more accessible contracts that would empower local communities to help themselves as well as more locally accountable and multi-dimensional funding sources. Subsidiarity would also require certain activities to be implemented by congregations, while others might need to occur at the level of the diocese or a regional or national body yet to be formed.

Furthermore, this principle would mean three main things in practice. First, the size and ferocity of contracts, the contradictory nature of their specifications and/or the irregularity of their payments should be examined and curbed, lest they destroy the voluntary ethos of third sector bodies. Second, the local state should divide contracts

---

131   United States Catholic Bishops (1986) *Economic Justice for All: A Pastoral Letter on Catholic Social Teaching and the U.S. Economy*, USCC: Washington.

to maximise the number of voluntary sector entrants to government markets. Thirdly – linked to the concept of 'gift' – contracts should allow for the development of 'extra value' criteria, including user empowerment and advocacy in order to hold Government to its task of 'assisting'. Rt Hon Ed Miliband MP said that 'if hugged by a politician, the third sector should be suspicious and 'check its pockets'.[132] The principle of subsidiarity would seek to repair relations between Government and the voluntary sector, while strengthening the sector independence that Miliband spoke of in the same speech. Much though remains to be done.

4.4 Civic Value Matrix

Developing the Christian principles for commissioning mentioned above is one key priority, particularly as they will provide ground upon which Church leaders and others across the country can enter into a conversation as to the manner and form of contracting in, by and with the local and regional state. Such principles can also inform episcopal contributions at the national level. In this section we offer a 'working model' to help Church groups called the 'Civic Value' matrix. We are happy for this matrix to be used on an 'open source' basis as long as proper attribution is given. As we continue to develop this tool, we will welcome feedback on its relevance on all levels.

Our research has suggested that the Church needs to steer a middle path between intense enthusiasm for public action grounded on non-existent resources and overburdened souls, and apathetic gradualism sustained by significant assets and overwhelming *politesse*. Christians need to discover and reinvent the 'mission shaped church' as much in the sphere of social action and engagement as in any other area of mission.

Therefore, a prior set of judgements must be made by those seeking to engage – judgements that will require debate, prayer, discernment and inspiration. These judgements respond to identified needs and ought to have a relationship to capacity and a relational consistency between theology, ecclesiology, capacity and desired contribution.

The 'Civic Value' matrix is not intended to be a tool to help measure the impact of Christian service or witness. Rather, it is intended to serve as a framework by which those at their appropriate level in the Church can frame their decision-making as to whether and how they may respond to needs or be civically engaged. Principles and

---

132 Rt Hon E. Miliband MP (2008) 'Partners Not Rivals: Civil Society and the State' NCVO Conference.

values are linked to operational capacity, skills, assets, etc. that are at hand or can be found in a strategic partnership.

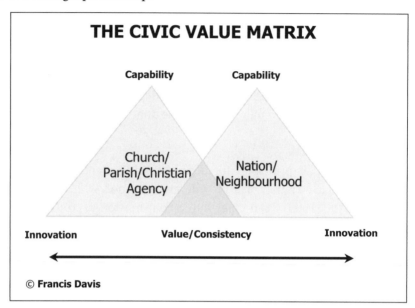

THE CIVIC VALUE MATRIX

Capability   Capability

Church/Parish/Christian Agency   Nation/Neighbourhood

Innovation   Value/Consistency   Innovation

© Francis Davis

Locating Church:
The triangle on the left of the diagram represents the part of the church where you are located. Is this a parish? A diocese? A group within a parish or diocese? A national charity or a new community initiative? By locating where we are 'church', we can then be clear about what resources we can call upon and what scope our existing or new work will have.

Locating the Place:
Are we focused on a neighbourhood or a particular kind of need? Is the 'place' we are concerned with the geographical boundaries of the diocese or the nation? Or do we wish to focus on some form of international need?

Discerning Innovation:
To be Christian is to live with change. To what extent does our initiative meet unmet needs? To what extent does it mirror successful projects from elsewhere? Are we starting afresh? By determining whether we are being truly innovative will help us plan resources and identify spiritual material to sustain us.

Do we want to consider partnering with Government? Or would we rather 'go it alone'? Shall we work with another voluntary body? Are we advocates or carers?

Assessing Capability:

To what extent is our vision of the Church matched by the size of the 'place' that we have taken on? Do we have the right skills in terms of fundraising, finance, and coordination? Do we need buildings, grants, or lawyers? What networks do we have to increase our capacity? What judgements do we have to make about how balanced our planning group is? Is everyone a 'doer' or are we all 'thinkers'? If so, how might we balance things out, and when is the best time to bring new people on board?

Consistency and Value:

To ensure consistency of principles it will be necessary to agree on the relative importance of evangelism by word and social action, and on the principles of governance that may have to be put in place. This might include studying funding agreements signed by other bodies in order to understand their likely implications for church and place.

The 'value' is the means by which you plan to record what you consider to be important in the project's ongoing work and achievements. It should reflect your consistent theological and spiritual principles.

PART 5: CONCLUSION AND RECOMMENDATIONS

The absence of an evidence base on the Church's huge moral and civic contribution – and the seeming lack of interest in even seriously considering it – has meant that the state is planning without vision or roots and not even recognising its own creed of 'what works'. Unless something changes, this will undermine a far larger part of our civic health than has been imagined at a time when all parties are saying that the 'little platoons' of society are vital.

This report raises issues of considerable importance. We have encountered a Church that had been under the (mistaken) impression that it was well understood in Government, and a government that is highly limited in its understanding of the Church.

Alongside Christians who were volunteering beyond the norm, establishing new models of Church and welfare service, and doing so most often without recognition, we met some Church leaders and activists whose view of the welfare state remains firmly planted in the past century. With this deeply held but historically static vision of welfarism, they had been unable to tease out many of the new areas of concern and governance that now define policy debate, especially with regard to the poorest. Their passion is obviously motivating and can help to sustain important work at the local level. However, in the face of social change the old frameworks and battles that they knew and understood have been shattered, perhaps making them more conservative than they had realised.

The possibility now is to forge a new hopeful future beyond misperceptions, misjudgements and crises in evidence. It is with this hope in mind that we now turn to our recommendations and final remarks.

5.1 Recommendations
Despite our hesitation to make any formal recommendations, bishops and several Members of Parliament urged us to do so, suggesting that we develop proposals that would be addressed to multiple areas of both Church and state. We aimed not to generate a 'fixed menu' of areas for improvement, but rather an 'à la carte menu' that could provide a framework for further conversation, research and possible action in this arena.

As we have written this report to the Church *and* the nation, we have broken our recommendations down into those intended for consideration by Government and those intended for consideration by the Church. It should be stressed that these recommendations arise from reflection upon the suggestions, ideas, comments and proposals that we encountered during the research process. Like the Christian principles for commissioning mentioned previously, these recommendations reflect the values and aspirations of those whom we have met in the course of this study and in this sense they are forged at the coalface of pastoral care and social practice.

5.1.1 TO NUMBER 10

(i) That the Government fundamentally review its commissioning guidance and policies across every domestic department of state with a mind to developing fresh directions that emphasise decentralisation of contracts, as well as the importance of advocacy, non economic performance measurements and long term 'covenant' relationships in commissioning.

(ii) That the Government introduce new legislation to create a level playing field for faith-based agencies seeking to engage in public service reform, contracting and civic action.

(iii) That the Government name a Minister for Religion, Social Cohesion and Voluntary Action (who also would serve as the Prime Minister's direct faith envoy) to recognise the striking contribution of the faith communities more structurally across *every* department of state from the MOD to the DWP. While we praise Rt Hon Stephen Timms MP for his work in this area, we argue that faith communities merit more than just a *party* post under the new Prime Minister. They should have both a Vice Chair and a Minister.

5.1.2 TO THE CABINET OFFICE

(i) That once the contract for the new Cabinet Office's centre of research/evidence excellence in the third sector has been awarded, several departments of state should provide additional funds to develop a serious and extended faith-based evidence strand of research, including a robust look at the wide-ranging civic contribution of the Churches. This should include studies of the role of 'theology' and 'spirituality' as key motivational languages and theories of engagement and organisation.

(ii)   That this strand of research should include identifying social innovations invented and founded by the Churches internationally, which are ripe for policy transfer. The Department for Children, Schools and Families, for example, has recently borrowed its 'Studio Schools' model from an approach to truancy pioneered by Church groups in the Bronx (USA).

(iii)   That the National School of Government (or a similar body), as part of the renewal of government skills and knowledge in this area, should be funded by several departments to develop a 'Religion, Governance, Public Policy and Management' executive programme in close partnership with the Churches. This programme should form part of senior civil service and voluntary sector umbrella network training.

(iv)   That the Cabinet Office should increase its interdisciplinary and cross-cutting specialist strengths in the religious voluntary sector and strengthen the relationship with faith communities across every department of state.

5.1.3 TO THE CHARITY COMMISSION

(i)   That the Charity Commission should review and amend its classification criteria so that Ministers have a meaningful evidence base on Churches and other faith communities from which to plan.

(ii)   That the Charity Commission open a sustained period of dialogue with the largest Christian denominations in the UK, especially those in the membership of the Churches Together in Britain and Ireland, and that this should include regional and national as well as congregational voices.

5.1.4 TO THE FOREIGN OFFICE AND DFID

(i)   That HM Ambassador to the Holy See and the UK Permanent Representative to the European Commission should work with the Anglican Centre in Rome and the Conference of European Churches to facilitate a major international conference on the UK and Commonwealth experience of public service re-form, the role of the Anglican Church and other faith communities in that process, and their wider service and advocacy with and for the poor.

(ii)   That DFID fund a small group of Christian NGO policy departments to collaborate on a report showcasing best practice in working with Christian NGOs in overseas settings with a mind to replication on the UK home front.

5.1.5 TO THE ARCHBISHOPS OF CANTERBURY AND YORK

(i)   That public service reform and the Church's role in domestic welfare provision be the subject of a workshop at the forthcoming Lambeth Conference.

(ii)   That the Archbishops call a St George's House consultation (or its equivalent) to follow up on some of our interim findings.

(iii) That the Archbishops commission a feasibility study to establish a new Lambeth- and York-led 'Anglican Philanthropy' fund to encourage a fresh wave of donors to back Christian social innovation, advocacy and welfare provision with both funding and the investment of time, skills and knowledge in a strategic and coordinated fashion.

(iv)   That the Archbishop of Canterbury, in conversation with Lambeth Partners, should explore the establishment of annual 'Archbishop's Awards for Faith-Based Civic Action,' ideally in partnership with a national umbrella body such as ACEVO and with the media. These awards would celebrate and recognise the role and contribution of faith-based social innovation, service and action across the country. They would affirm not only inter-faith conversation, but also the full realm of faith-based civic contributions.

5.1.6 TO THE LORDS SPIRITUAL

(i)   That our interim findings form the basis for a debate in the House of Lords to examine the weaknesses we have uncovered in the Government's approach to the Churches, as well as the wider need for a refreshed set of contracting principles, which are rooted in an attempt to measure more qualitative factors and enable a wider range of sustainable voluntary sector engagement.

5.1.7 TO THE HOUSE OF BISHOPS & THE GENERAL SYNOD

(i)   That the Church should establish a new social enterprise/voluntary sector support and coordinating body to develop public advocacy and service provision engagement across the country, modelled on existing best practice in its work in education and on international counterparts such as Anglicare in Australia. This body would encourage the support and continued development of the existing Anglican contributions to health and social care, community development, post-compulsory education, criminal justice, asylum and refugee advice and services, welfare-to-work, job creation, the rural economy and the arts and cultural economy. It would also encourage increased utilisation and coordination of activities in the civic hubs of cathedrals and dioceses. It may have some ecumenical potential as well, since some of the Catholic children's societies are seeking, or are being required, to reinvent themselves outside the governance networks of the Roman Catholic Church.

(ii)   That the Church develop a fresh conversation and process of theological enquiry as to the appropriate nature, form and content of Christian principles for contracting. This could include bishops addressing these 'principles' while visiting chief executives in their diocesan areas or while engaging in their myriad civic activities. It could also include a sustained campaign alongside smaller voluntary organisations to enhance decentralisation of contracts and increase wider civic engagement.

5.1.8 TO THEOLOGICAL COLLEGES / MINISTERIAL TRAINING PROGRAMMES

(i)   That coursework introducing the modern structure of the state (including commissioning, the role of the voluntary sector, and the nature and form of public management and its successors) become a mandatory part of ministerial training.

(ii)   That pioneering projects at local, diocesan, and Anglican Communion levels are regularly 'case studied' in ministerial training as a source of inspiration and creative thinking and as a reminder of the Church's innovative nature.

(iii)   That training in grant and bid writing, as well as performance leadership, be available to Ordinands.

5.2 Final Remarks

In the course of our research for this report, we have encountered a Church of England that, proportionate to its size, makes extensive contributions to the civic health of the nation. Bishops engage in countless activities ranging from involvement in fundraising appeals, to regeneration, to sitting on governing bodies of local schools or colleges, to community leadership. Cathedrals serve a dual role of being centres of prayer and of great potential for social action, education and regeneration – all within a rich Christian narrative of 'hospitality' and 'openness'. Dioceses contain significant resources, both financial and human, that could enable them to become meaningful players in welfare provision and the strengthening of community foundations. Congregations, with their unique ability to know and understand the situation locally, have shown a true spirit of innovation in their quest to meet the needs presented (i.e. opening a post office in church) and to raise funds for wider Christian social innovations in housing, addiction, family support and anti-poverty campaigning. In this sense, it is no wonder that Anglican organisations and institutions have been pioneers and leaders in development work, children's needs, and every area of civil society. All in all, the Church of England has proven itself to have the conviction, institutional capacity, innovative spirit and skills to extend its current reach even more widely, should it so wish. This will be a moment for leadership in the Church.

Yet, despite this immense and longstanding involvement by the Anglican Church, the government, with notable exceptions, has consistently failed to pay more than enthusiastic lip service to its role in society generally and in the third sector in particular.

In turn this means that Government is being experienced at the local and national level in negative ways. Its perceived discrimination against the Christian Church and other religious bodies, coupled with the relative downgrading of regional and other local actors, suggests a policy-making environment that has essentially excluded, or pushed to the margins, social voices (not just religious ones) that are vital to civic debate. Those whom we met felt that the social welfare contracting regime as presently constituted must be reshaped in light of these concerns.

It is clear that the Conservatives have, at the least, a *rhetorical* desire to address many of these issues. In the case of the Labour Government, that intention is not so clear despite, as we have said, the outstanding efforts of a few Ministers and MPs. The prevailing culture of the government seems to flow against these principled pioneers.

Bearing all of this in mind, it is unsurprising that our respondents in the Church and Parliament, from the regions to London, in business and academia, told us that a fresh dialogue was needed. Such a fresh conversation, supported by new research and a new commitment on the part of both the Church and government to mobilise resources, could lead to inventive new work alongside the poorest and neediest in the UK and abroad.

This fresh dialogue should start with the open and enthusiastic recognition of what the Church already does in every county and constituency in the country. It should start with a new covenant of mutual respect. As one clergyperson emphasised, 'real toleration and human rights are rooted in community and a certain openness of mind, not mutual ignorance'. Both Church and state must become more receptive of the other.

Only if such a fresh conversation emerges will the government manage to steer its faith-based policies back on course, and the Church step forward once again with a new confidence for the times. Only then will the government truly recover a convincing moral direction and its badly needed compass.

APPENDIX A

The Faithworks Charter

Principles for Churches and local Christian agencies committed to excellence in community work and service provision in the UK

Motivated by our Christian faith we _____ commit ourselves to the following standards as we serve others in our community work and seek to model trust.

Signed _____   Date _____

Position _____

We will provide an inclusive service to our community by:

1.   Serving and respecting all people regardless of their gender, marital status, race, ethnic origin, religion, age, sexual orientation or physical and mental capability.

2.   Acknowledging the freedom of people of all faiths or none both to hold and to express their beliefs and convictions respectfully and freely, within the limits of the UK law.

3.   Never imposing our Christian faith or belief on others.

4.   Developing partnerships with other churches, voluntary groups, statutory agencies and local government wherever appropriate in order to create an effective, integrated service for our clients avoiding unnecessary duplication of resources.

5.   Providing and publicising regular consultation and reporting forums to client groups and the wider community regarding the effective development and delivery of our work and our responsiveness to their actual needs.

We will value all individuals in a way that is consistent with our distinctive Christian ethos by:

1.   Creating an environment where clients, volunteers and employees are encouraged and enabled to realise their potential.

2.   Assisting our clients, volunteers and employees to take responsibility for their own learning and development, both through formal and informal training opportunities and ongoing assessment.

3.   Developing an organisational culture in which individuals learn from any mistakes made and where excellence and innovation are encouraged and rewarded.

4.   Promoting the value of a balanced, holistic lifestyle as part of each individual's overall personal development.

5.   Abiding by the requirements of employment law in the UK and implementing best employment practices and procedures designed to maintain our distinctive ethos and values.

We will develop a professional approach to management, practice and funding by:

1.   Implementing a management structure, which fosters and encourages participation by staff at all levels in order to facilitate the fulfillment of the project's goals and visions.

2.   Setting and reviewing measurable and timed outcomes annually, and regularly to evaluate and monitor our management structure and output, recognising the need for ongoing organisational flexibility, development and good stewardship of resources.

3.   Doing all we can to ensure that we are not over-dependent on any one source of funding.

4.   Implementing best practice procedures in terms of Health and Safety and Child Protection in order to protect our staff, volunteers and clients.

5.   Handling our funding in a transparent and accountable way and to give relevant people from outside our organisation/project reasonable access to our accounts.

© *Faithworks (administered by the Oasis Charitable Trust) 2002*

APPENDIX B

Interim Briefing to Parmjit Dhanda MP

On 29th April 2008 the following briefing on this report was provided to the DCLG ahead of a planned meeting between Bishop Stephen Lowe and Parmjit Dhanda MP. After the briefing was sent, Mr Dhanda's office cancelled.

REPORT BY THE VON HÜGEL INSTITUTE FOR THE ARCHBISHOPS' COUNCIL OF THE CHURCH OF ENGLAND

Francis Davis, Elizabeth Paulhus, Andrew Bradstock

1. Ours has been an exploratory study. Its basic conclusion is that while the government's faith-based agenda means well, and is backed by individuals of integrity, enthusaism and skill, it lacks nuance and rich insight despite the best efforts of these individuals. In turn this is likely in the long run to hamper the faith sector's civic contribution in general and that of the Christian Churches – and especially the Church of England – in particular. This lack of nuance is significantly enhanced by omissions in the work of the Charity Commission and goes right to the heart of debates regarding English identity.

2. The study will be developed in further studies in the EEDA and SEEDA areas and in a series of special editions of academic journals, and will be disseminated in mainstream and religious media. We will also be running regional study days with local bishops and policy makers and will welcome invitations to government and sector-sponsored events.

3. Our report is based on interviews and workshops involving over 200 bishops, community activists, voluntary sector leaders, parliamentarians and academics. We also ran a private discussion dinner for leading charity chief executives.

4. We have additionally undertaken new empirical work to look at (i) the institutional capacity of the Church of England at the diocesan/regional level; and (ii) the civic contribution of bishops. We also describe local Church projects involving police stations, post offices, GP surgeries, dental surgeries, social enterprises, and business incubator units in church buildings and the economic and civic contribution of cathedrals. We note that many of the country's leading social entrepreneurs have their roots and core social networks in faith-based social innovation and especially Christian social innovation.

5. We collect both published and unpublished data to assist the Government – and the Church - to begin to gather fresh evidence relating to the work of the Church as a whole. We are concerned that the Government's approach to engaging with churches appears to comprise a mix of 'silo mentalities' and a failure to acquire appropriate data. This is the first time that such data will be gathered across the various departments within the Church of England. We also uncover (a) misperceptions on the part of the Church as to what it understood by the 'commissioning state'; and (b) huge omissions in the statutory approach to faith communities in general and the Church of England in particular.

6. We unpack the direction of travel of both Government and Opposition on public service reform/developing a responsible society. We note the possible threat to Anglican charities contained in what we were told is the Government's expressed intention to adopt Lords/Commons proposals to extend the Human Rights Act by making Anglican charities 'public authorities' if they are in receipt of state funds.

7. Three departments of state told us that Government had *no* evidence base with regard to the various Christian churches, and the Cabinet Office was surprised by the very idea that this might be desirable/necessary for policy making. The largest religious body in the country – the Church of England - has been ommitted from these studies quite specifically. This contrasted heavily with the evidence base that we uncovered for minority faith communities as part of the government's anti-radicalisation and charity governance improvement agenda. We were consequently unsurprised that some minority faith communities felt 'victimised' by the Charity Commission.

8. The Commission does not know how many faith-based organisations there are in England and Wales. Its figures fail to capture any Anglican parishes, and this situation will not change considerably even after the implementation of the new Charity Act. Moreover, problems of classification mean that many faith-based organisations – especially Christian ones – are not seen as such because they are registered to 'relieve poverty', not for 'religious activities'. Hence, Church Action on Poverty, Housing Justice and the St Vincent de Paul Society would not be counted in any assessment of the churches' contribution to the nation, despite their explicitly Christian nature. In one unpublished academic estimate that we have read, it is suggested that the number of Christian organisations is underestimated by over 50%.

The Cabinet Office is certainly right when it says that the Office of National Statistics serves the voluntary sector badly. Such a lack of evidence is striking given the roots of English identity and distorts attitudes to the Churches and faith communities in the central civil service and local government.

If the Commission's current consultation document on the meaning of 'public benefit' were implemented, the situation could worsen further. Its application of a limited view of religiosity could stifle current Church campaigning against the Burmese junta (against the national interest?) and may have thwarted various Christian activity in the past, such as developing the Jubilee Debt Campaign ('quoting a sacred text for political purposes') or funding the legal costs of the Rivonia Trial defendants in apartheid South Africa (not advancing religion?). It may also have hampered the development by religious groups of the inter-faith 'Living Wage' campaign (founded on a religious retreat), which Rt Hon Ed Miliband MP claimed as a victory for the Labour government at Labour's recent spring conference.

9. A consequence of this is that all departments of state interacting with the third sector are underestimating the capabilities and skills of some religious bodies – and especially the Church of England – when it comes to the development of advocacy, service delivery and social cohesion. A relatively partial reading of social capital theory seems to have led the civil service to compare unlike with unlike across faith communities (with detrimental effects on some bodies in some regions, which have been asked to do too much relative to their size and have ended up doing nothing due to 'engagement fatigue'). The Church of England comprises, but is bigger than its 'congregations' and can operate at more than grassroots level.

10. Given this gap in data and the reliance of policy-makers on research drawn from independent evangelical, Muslim and Jewish experience, it is not surprising that the direction of policy travel at DCLG and FaithAction, for example, is towards 'congregational' and grassroots attempts to address social inclusion, the development of advocacy and service provision. While this may not be unwise in some instances, in general it fails to recognise the variety of institutional structures in religious denominations and the 'what works' model of Anglican dioceses, all bar one of which have committed to the Academies programme and all of which run other schools and community projects. Our empirical data show them to have highly skilled staff, along with networks and

net assets that surpass the networks, skills and assets of any current religious umbrella body and even of some (less than sympathetic) secular national umbrella bodies too. While in the Christian world we admire Faithworks it is smaller than every Anglican diocese and some Anglican parishes.

11. It should be noted that *all* of our religious respondents remarked on the Government's faith illiteracy, especially with regard to its inclination to reduce religion to an 'idea' (71.8% telling the Census office that they believe in a Christian God) as opposed to a way of life that involves institution building and social action (the religiously observant are 50% more likely to volunteer than secular neighbours according to the Home Office).

Particularly strong reservations were expressed regarding the attitude and openness of local authorities and other parts of the local state such as the NHS. One former DFID senior civil servant told us, 'he had been astonished to see how hard it was to work with the state on the domestic front'.

APPENDIX C

Round the Cabinet: Exemplar community-based projects funded by Anglican resources in Cabinet Ministers' Constituencies

The following case studies were provided by the Church Urban Fund (CUF) to illustrate the wide range of work undertaken by the Church of England (and other faith communities) within the constituencies of Cabinet members. The case studies have been chosen by CUF as 'best practice' examples of Church engagement in the wider community. We have accepted them at face value as the study did not permit time to evaluate all of them.

As CUF only funds projects in England, no examples are given for those Cabinet members with constituencies in Northern Ireland, Wales and Scotland. Additionally, CUF currently does not fund projects in the constituencies of Ashfield (Rt Hon Geoff Hoon MP), Leigh (Rt Hon Andy Burnham MP), Redditch (Rt Hon Jacqui Smith MP), or Bolton West (Rt Hon Ruth Kelly MP).

Rt Hon Ed Balls MP, Normanton
Woodhouse Community Centre
The Woodhouse Estate in Normanton suffers from a number of problems, many of which were triggered by the collapse of the mining industry and its ensuing economic decline. Problems include high unemployment and poor educational achievement. The local church has invested in using its building as a means to help tackle these problems, renovating and making it more user-friendly so that a variety of activities can be offered to local residents. Its central location in the estate means that the building is a good meeting point for residents who wish to take advantage of its multi-purpose focus. The centre offers adult education, training in literacy and numeracy and basic computer skills. CUF has assisted in the development of this project through its grants programme, which helped facilitate the necessary renovations to the church building.

Rt Hon Hilary Benn MP, Leeds Central
The Manuel Bravo Project
On 15 September 2005, an asylum seeker named Manuel Bravo committed suicide in a detention centre prior to his deportation. He had been forced to represent himself in court when his London solicitor failed to attend. In his memory, this project in central Leeds works with asylum seekers and refugees by offering support and legal advice in their asylum claims.

At a time when many asylum seekers and refugees find it difficult to access the necessary help to assist in their claims, and when they often suffer from a lack of legal representation, this project has sought to fill this gap in provision. *Manuel Bravo* seeks to ensure that cases are reviewed, provides help in preparing cases with appropriate evidence and information on the legal system, supports female asylum seekers who have been raped and are intimidated by the criminal justice process, and refers cases to necessary service providers.

This project has significantly helped to reduce the number of asylum seekers attending MPs' surgeries and the Citizens Advice Bureau, as well as to reduce the number of those who are destitute in the city. The project supports legal service providers in Leeds who have inadequate capacity to deal with their current caseload. *Manuel Bravo* operates on the support of volunteers from churches and the universities who are well trained to sustain this valuable work. CUF funding helps employ the Project Manager.

The Joanna Project

The Joanna Project is based in central Leeds and was established in 2004 to respond to the needs of prostitutes in Leed's red light district. Built upon a belief that relationships are essential to helping women build self-esteem and self-worth, the project aims to help women access professional services and encourages them to leave prostitution. An outreach team goes into Leeds two evenings a week with a 'mobile drop-in', which provides a temporary safe haven where friendships are built and a listening ear can be found. Wholesome sandwiches, fresh fruit, hot drinks, chocolates, homemade cakes and pampering packs are also distributed, along with personal safety information. This evening outreach is a good first point of contact with local prostitutes, 95% of whom have had contact with the mobile drop-in.

Day time work includes meeting with some of the women to discuss issues on a one-to-one basis and offering practical help with accommodation, counselling, drug treatment, financial management, health, pregnancy support, training and education. This project has strong Christian links and receives support from CUF to employ the project manager.

Rt Hon Hazel Blears MP, Salford

REVIVE

The Greater Manchester area has witnessed an increasing number of asylum seekers and refugees in recent years. REVIVE provides support and advice to individuals and their families, particularly if they require legal assistance. Furthermore, the project seeks to raise awareness of the issues facing asylum seekers in order to provide training for churches wishing to develop services in this area.

As the number of refugees and asylum seekers in Greater Manchester has grown, the need for paid workers likewise has increased. With the help of funding from CUF, REVIVE has been able to employ a Project Manager who is responsible for the day-to-day administration, including the management of volunteers. Additionally, the project manager provides a professional service of advocacy, orientation and psychological support for service users.

Rt Hon Yvette Cooper MP, Pontefract and Castleford
Saviour Youth
The Saviour Youth project is located in Pontefract, which still suffers from the decline of the mining industry. Problems include alcohol abuse, family breakdown, health inequality, poor educational achievement and pockets of concentrated deprivation. Some would describe the community as tight-knit, whilst others would argue it is 'insular'.

Saviour Youth grew out of the Youth Group at All Saints Church, Pontefract, to work with young people and to provide a safe and enjoyable meeting place for them. The project offers drop-ins, trips out, educational activities, homework clubs, gardening, football, crafts clubs, and advice on issues such as alcohol, drugs and sexual health.

The project has developed its work into four branches: YouthMax aims to broaden aspirations and horizons, YouthSoccer uses sport as a means to build self-esteem and confidence, YouthNext-Door builds community through detached youth work, and YouthValued works on a one-to-one basis to tackle specific issues. Funding from CUF has supported this work, allowing Saviour Youth to provide staff training, salaries and the equipment needed to sustain this work amongst the most socially excluded and deprived.

All Saints' Community Centre
All Saints, linked with the Saviour Youth Project, has been a centre for community activities since its establishment in the 1930s. Whilst a good space with the potential to offer a variety of facilitates for the benefit of the community, the building was in disrepair and thus was unable to continue to offer its services to the community. Activities had to move location, thereby reducing the numbers served because of the distance that had to be travelled. After undertaking a social audit, the general consensus among the public was that the church was needed as a community meeting point because it served as the

only true community facility in the area. Thus the refurbishment, facilitated by CUF funding, has helped to restore a building for the benefit of the community.

Rt Hon John Denham MP, Southampton, Itchen
SCRATCH, Basics Bank

Southampton City Mission founded SCRATCH (Southampton City and Region Action to Combat Hardship) as a Christian project to help develop numerous activities throughout the city, including a furniture project, recycling and a Christmas toy project. Through these activities SCRATCH has made contact with over 13,500 people in Southampton.

Working in conjunction with this project is the 'Basics Bank' initiative, which offers emergency food and clothing to people through a referral system. Over 100 local agencies hand out special vouchers indicating what assistance is required and who has referred the person. Despite relatively low unemployment, this area of Southampton has a number of people on low wages, as well as refugees and asylum seekers who require help.

Support for this project comes from volunteers from a number of churches and faith organisations, including Churches Together, Evangelical Alliance, Christian Aid Network and the Council of Faiths. CUF has supported this project by enabling the employment of the Basics Bank coordinator so that the project can become sustainable and reach its potential in the provision of food and clothing.

The Caretaker's House

When the head teacher of St Mark's Primary School in Southampton wanted to tackle the problem identified by the diocese of failing to deal with children's spirituality, the caretaker's house at the local school was converted into a venue for children's church. It was then developed into a venue that could be used for a variety of activities including parent support, parenting skills, coffee mornings and football clubs.

Furthermore, financial support from CUF has been used towards the funding of a worker who has established links with other organisations to offer debt, marriage and parenting counselling, as well as family supervised access and targeted services for women whose partners are in prison. The worker has been able to network with other agencies to offer an array of services to the local community. St Mark's Church has been heavily involved with the development of this project through the provision of volunteers, as the activities of the Caretaker's House have been integrated into the wider activities of the church community.

Rt Hon Harriet Harman MP, Camberwell and Peckham
PUMPS (Peckham Urban Mission Placement Scheme)
PUMPS is affiliated with All Saints Church, located in a culturally and ethnically diverse community in Peckham. The local population comprises 28% under the age of sixteen, and the project focuses upon this cohort. The lay assistants, or 'pumps', work in the local area with young people on a variety of projects. In addition, 70 volunteers from the church congregation assist by working with over 600 children and 350 young people through holiday schemes, Saturday clubs, school projects, baby clubs and a parent and toddler group.

This project works with the local police who view it as a positive asset to the community because it has helped to reduce crime and offers young people an alternative way of life. The 'pumps' also benefit through two years of training and experience. All Saints Church is integral to the running of this project, and CUF funding has helped to refurbish the church building and to cover some of the general operating costs.

Rt Hon John Hutton MP, Barrow and Furness
St John's Community Artspace and Social Area
Barrow Island is an area of extreme deprivation with few opportunities for local residents to develop educational or employment skills. St John's Church observed the need to offer a holistic means of helping people develop skills through participating in activities which make them feel comfortable.

St John's had a large building with the potential to become a community centre that could provide room for various social groups. With funding from CUF, amongst others, the building was renovated to create additional multipurpose space. As one of the only community spaces available in which to run activities, the strategic importance of the building is significant.

This community centre now offers recreational, social, leisure and educational activities. For example, the Artspace provides the opportunity for a community artist to work with the local school and develop additional services aimed at all members of the community.

Rt Hon Alan Johnson MP, Kingston upon Hull West and Hessle
Hull Youth for Christ (YFC)
Situated in an area struggling with high levels of crime and deviancy, poor educational achievement, high levels of unemployment, and social problems including drug and

alcohol misuse, teenage pregnancies, violent crime and gang activities, YFC offers young people supportive recreation and education opportunities through which they gain new experiences. This ensures that young people better participate in community life which in turn enhances citizenship.

YFC is viewed favourably by the local authority because of the positive impact it has had upon crime rates. Furthermore, because YFC is a national organisation, the project is linked to many churches across Hull. CUF has helped support this venture by enabling the employment of a youth worker who builds relationships with local young people through which these services can be tailored to local needs.

Rt Hon David Miliband MP, South Shields
South Tyneside Churches' Key Project
South Tyneside is an area still enduring the legacy of economic decline and deindustrialisation which has led to high unemployment, poor literacy and numeracy and a failure to replace the lost jobs with jobs of similar skill and pay levels. The Key Project seeks to tackle these problems of deprivation amongst the young people (16-25) of South Tyneside who are facing hardships with drug and alcohol problems, low skilled jobs, a lack of aspiration, high rates of teenage pregnancy and/ or homelessness.

The project seeks to provide young people with social networks through which relationships can be built and through which they can be referred to specialist services pertaining to tenancy, employment, health and education. The Key Project links with other service providers in order to deal with problems in a holistic manner. Churches Together in South Tyneside, comprising 70 churches, helps support this project through providing finances, volunteers, in-kind contributions, premises and management committee members. CUF has funded the post of an Administration and Finance Officer who makes sure that the project runs as smoothly as possible.

Rt Hon Ed Miliband MP, Doncaster North
Doncaster Communities Live at Home Scheme
Whilst the activities of this project are focused upon central Doncaster, the reach of them extends across the whole city. The scheme aims to provide a range of services to older people (aged 60+) living in their own homes. The services help older people maintain their independence, reduce social isolation, improve confidence levels and learn new skills. This work is supported by volunteers who sustain three weekly drop-in sessions with activity programmes, as well as undertaking volunteer visiting and

transporting older people to appointments, helping with shopping and banking, and taking the users on social outings. The project is run in conjunction with a local church and has been supported by CUF funding that has been used towards the salaries of two part-time staff. This project is significant in ensuring that the needs of the elderly are not marginalised and that their exclusion is prevented.

Rt Hon James Purnell MP, Stalybridge and Hyde
Parish Nurse Project

Hyde has experienced severe economic decline since its industrial base collapsed during the 1970s-1980s. Although some of the former cotton and tobacco mills have been converted into small business units, the area predominately affords low-skilled, low-wage employment. Industrial disease incidences are prevalent, and with no doctors' surgeries in the locality, health issues are a particular problem for the area.

The parishes of St Mary, St Thomas and St Stephen saw the need to employ a parish nurse who is able to provide holistic and continuous care for local residents. The parish nurse trains volunteers so that the geographical reach of the services provided can be maximised, concentrating especially on the areas suffering from the poorest access to health care. Strong relationships have been built not only between churches, but also with statutory bodies. CUF has helped develop this project through its grants programme, which assisted in the recruitment of the parish nurse who now provides spiritual, physical and emotional health care to communities previously lacking such basic necessities.

Rt Hon Jack Straw MP, Blackburn
St Luke's Church Development Worker

This project is located in an area of Blackburn struggling with high unemployment, drug related crime and little integration of the white and Asian communities. Whilst classed as a 'regeneration zone' by local authorities, the social fabric is still undermined by the aforementioned issues. In conjunction with the police, local schools, SureStart, the local college and the wider community, St Luke's Church undertook a community consultation that revealed a desire to use the church hall as a multicultural community resource centre.

The building is used by the local school for activities and also serves as the venue for regeneration zone meetings, a café, training classes and the MP's surgery. St Luke's has employed an Arts Development Worker who has developed a programme of activities, which seeks to promote holistic social and spiritual values and to facilitate a cross-cultural experience. CUF has contributed towards the salary of the development worker whose work encourages participative involvement and community cohesion.

Blackburn Cathedral's Asylum Seeker and Refugee project

Blackburn has experienced an increase in the number of refugees, mainly from Africa, settling in the area. There has been increasing social segregation between the Muslim and wider communities, and gangs have formed in opposition over specific issues. Consequently, many refugees seek support in the cathedral and local churches from targeted violence and oppression.

In response to the many issues arising, Blackburn Cathedral has employed a worker who supports refugees and asylum seekers, and also lobbies, challenges perceptions and educates people on the issues being faced by this minority community. The Cathedral is perfectly placed to help because it is open every day and is naturally a place in which people would seek refuge and solace. The Asylum Seeker and Refugee Project is supported by Churches Together, with some funding from CUF towards the employment of the worker.

Rt Hon Shaun Woodward MP, St Helens South

ROC (St Helens Homeless Centre)

St Helens has many homeless people or rough sleepers. Through its provision of services, the homeless centre seeks to meet the needs of those who are hard-to-reach or who have been deemed unacceptable by other agencies. The centre is open at night and provides laundry facilities, showers, health care and health advice, hairdressing, counselling, hot meals and an opportunity for social interaction. ROC has become a focal point for the homeless in St Helens, because it provides the only sheltered evening meal. Volunteers offer more than just food and basic provisions; they also reach out to the local people with compassion. CUF has assisted in the development of the ROC Homeless Centre by enabling the employment of a staff member who has facilitated the Centre's sustainability and the establishing of links with St Helens housing and homeless statutory sectors.

New Street Neighbourhood Development, St Helens

Based in the New Street Estate, this project seeks to engage with a community affected by high unemployment and social deprivation. Assisted by CUF funding, a Neighbourhood Worker has facilitated the building of links with local people to promote community involvement. Activities include an after-school club, a youth club, a furniture resource centre, and a tenants and residents' association. Whilst primarily serving the local community, this project also helps its volunteers develop their own potential through the training provided and the opportunities afforded for community involvement.

APPENDIX D

Regional Case Studies

i. Cathedrals at the heart of their communities

a. South West Cathedrals

An attempt in 2002 to measure the cultural investment represented by six cathedrals in the south west of England - Gloucester, Salisbury, Bristol, Wells, Exeter and Truro – found that much of the community involvement and cultural contribution is without any religious test; the cathedrals want to be seen as part of the region's cultural life; they currently give to the community more than they get from the government; and it should not be assumed that this pattern can continue indefinitely. The survey revealed that about £10m annually (2002 figures) is spent by the region's six cathedrals on cultural activities, half of which goes towards the costs of historic buildings, music, library/archives and education. Income from members, visitors and fundraising outstrips grants from public funds. Much expertise, and access to a significant number of events, is available to the public free or nearly free.

b. Canterbury

The schools department at Canterbury Cathedral processes and organises the visits of 95,000 school children from Britain and abroad each year. The children represent all faiths, and one particular London school, which includes many Sikh, Muslim and Hindu children, makes regular visits. The department works very actively with French schools.

c. Norwich

The Cathedral has used a Heritage Lottery Grant of c.£47k to create closer links with communities in the city and reach new visitors, breaking down some of the barriers and perceptions that meant that visitor numbers were low. Working with voluntary organisations, such as YMCA, and local social and adult education services, the cathedral now runs learning activities which bring the community together through involvement with its history, architecture and environment – for example, arts workshops are held on site involving photography, designing stained glass windows, making paper angels, working on a giant 'weave' and making large scale frescos and texture rubbings, all inspired by the cathedral. The scheme has attracted many new visitors into the cathedral to share its historical and cultural resources, a quarter of whom said they had never been there before.

d. Chelmsford

The education programme at the cathedral includes a variety of trails and activities. These are cross-curricular but designed to meet the needs of the National Curriculum, especially the Religious Education syllabus. Each visit may include exploring the main parts of the cathedral, using the senses, role-play, drawing, sketching and story telling. The day is planned in consultation with the requirements and special needs of the school. The children take an active part in each visit through role-play, dressing up, looking and finding and sketching. Each visit ends with a short act of worship at which a candle is lit for the school, the children and their prayers. During each Advent and Lent special workshops are held over four days to enable the children to focus on the Christian meaning of the festivals of Christmas and Easter, whilst having fun through music, drama, discovery, story telling, reflection and craft. In 2007 a special event called 'Free for All' was organised to commemorate the bicentenary of the abolition of the transatlantic slave-trade: this was the result of four special workshops which prepared this performance of drama, music and dance by local school.

e. St Albans

Each year St Albans Cathedral Education Centre welcomes 16,000 school visitors who participate in a variety of trails and workshops which complement the National Curriculum. Qualified teachers and specially trained volunteers lead small groups, helping them to uncover the past and explore the meanings and symbols of this centre of Christianity. The Centre works with all ages, faiths and abilities and welcome schools and youth groups from all over the UK and overseas. It has a Bursary Scheme, supported by a trust, to enable pupils from disadvantaged backgrounds to participate in all its activities. It strives to engender the ethos of 'Every Child Matters' through enjoying and achieving. The Centre's trails and practical workshops focus on the building and its history. Using role play, costume, objects and the building itself, pupils encounter the stories of St Albans Cathedral and are encouraged to 'become' worshippers from the past - humble monks, powerful bishops, silent Victorian children, Roman soldiers far from home or pilgrims at the end of a long journey. They may witness Alban's martyrdom, survive the Black Death, or rise in revolt. They may uncover hidden signs, make a mosaic or try to measure the building with a balloon. Special events are also held: for example, in November each year the Centre hosts a Sixth Form Conference when over 600 students debate current issues with a platform of high profile speakers using the BBC's 'Question Time' format. In January 2007 the cathedral hosted 'A Place For Poetry', providing Year 6 pupils with an opportunity to write poetry inspired by the building and its history.

ii. Eype Church Centre for the Arts (Dorset)

Supported by the Highland End Holiday Park, this church has been restored to serve as both as a place of worship and an art gallery and performance venue for use by holiday makers and local people.

iii. The Church of England in Rural Gloucestershire

In August 2002 the Gloucester Diocesan Rural Group commissioned research into the state of the rural church in the diocese. In an area where 60% of incumbents are responsible for between two and four churches, and 27% are responsible for five or more churches, the survey revealed that 75% of rural parish churches were open every day during daylight hours for prayer and quiet reflection. 45% are used at least once during the week for other activities as well as for Sunday worship. A total of 19 of the 155 parishes had no other building available for community use than their parish church.

56% of parochial church councils and 82% of incumbents said they would like to see church buildings used for a wide range of purposes that would benefit the local community – including children's activities, tourist information, counselling practices, doctors' surgeries, drop-in centres, cultural events and shops. The most positive responses came from parishes where the church building was already receiving regular use during the week. Comparing these findings with the responses to a similar survey in 1991 a senior cleric suggested that, 'while church buildings have always been valued, there is now a clear willingness on the part of local people to think flexibly and laterally, and an openness on their part to consider potential adaptations to the building.'

iv. Faith in the Black Country

A survey of faith communities across four areas in the Black Country found over 21,000 people actively working in their community as paid staff or volunteers – doing 2,500 full and part-time jobs; 26,000 hours of volunteer time given to community each week or 1,352,000 hours a year; 57,000 children and young people attending more than 2,000 youth activities; an investment of over £32 million a year in people resources; 3,500 community activities and projects, 77% open to anyone; 760 advice and guidance services such as debt counselling; and 777 practical help/skills projects such as food and furniture.

v. Faith in Oxfordshire

In 2004 the Bishop of Dorchester remarked: 'Many of us have come to realise that, because as Churches we have often failed to "tell our story" beyond our own congregations, it is not altogether surprising that we were ignored. Yet the fact remains that we, as faith communities, are the largest family of voluntary organisations in the Thames Valley, and our involvement in a wide spectrum of cultural activities is second to none.'

vi. Brighton

A survey of Christian organizations and voluntary groups in Brighton and Hove published in 2004 found 135 examples of individuals from a congregation volunteering for another voluntary or community group (ranging from hospitals to the Brighton Soup Run and the Samaritans); 92 examples of congregations and organisations running or contributing to community events and festivals such as 'fun-days', concerts, exhibitions and children's holiday clubs; 33 examples of congregations running a voluntary or community organisation or project in partnership with another group; and 301 examples of congregations and organisations running their own community activities, groups or projects. The services provided included advice and support, community space, training, health and cafes. Just 47% of these projects employ 134 staff, have 1072 volunteers and 6,300 users (including hirers).

vii. All Saints, Botley (Diocese of Portsmouth)

All Saints provides possibly the first example of a public library in a church. Situated in the foyer and run on a self-service basis, its books can be accessed whenever the church is open. No charges are made and it is entirely dependent on people's honesty. Hampshire Library Service visits regularly to change the stock. Whereas a mobile service may only visit a village once a week, and then for just a few hours, the community can now access the library most days, including some evenings and weekends. The county museums service has also installed a display cabinet in the church, housing material of local interest. This pilot 'Rural Discovery Centre' brings school groups and other local people into the church and will be developed as a partnership between the church, the Hampshire Library and Information Service, the Hampshire Museums Service and Eastleigh Borough Council. The church sees this as 'complementing and developing the current community use of the church', part of which involves an internet facility in a new extension with disabled access. This offers free access to the internet for anyone who comes in.

viii. Sacred Sussex

'Sacred Sussex' is a multi-faith tourism initiative in the Diocese of Chichester. It helps more than 300 churches and other places of worship to remain open and provides training and advice to help them ensure that tourists and local residents get value from their visit. Congregations are helped to develop innovative ways of attracting visitors and interpreting their heritage; develop educational opportunities; build partnerships with heritage and tourism organisations; and work with local businesses to boost the local economy. Funded by the Heritage Lottery Fund and the European Union, the project was initiated by the Diocese of Chichester and is run in partnership with West Sussex County Council, the Open Churches Partnership and Wealden District Council in partnership.

ix. Concerts in Churches

Started by the head of a company publishing church music, this initiative organises concerts in churches that are chosen for their general ambience, acoustic qualities and good facilities. Part of the challenge and motivation is to bring music to those areas which are off the musical map and usually ignored by outreach programmes. Begun in East Anglia, it is now nationwide.

x. Churches in Norwich

A survey in 2003 exploring the extent of the churches' social action in the City of Norwich showed that church volunteers provide 154,555 hours of social action per annum. This equates to 80 full-time jobs that would otherwise cost £740,000 (taking as the hourly rate the then minimum wage of £4.85). Services include drop-in centres, outreach work with the homeless, debt counselling and drug- and alcohol-user support. All are provided free.

xi. St Mark's Centre, Bedford (St Albans Diocese)

Situated in the Brickhill area of Bedford, St Mark's has been described as 'the beating heart of its community' for over 30 years. It is a surgery, a school, a police station and a church, as well as the host venue for nearly 50 community organisations. The centre has always made special provision for people with disabilities. In 2005 it was awarded European Social Funding to operate 'Clubhouse', a resource providing services and training for adults with learning disabilities who are disadvantaged in the labour market. It is a place to meet friends, have a meal and engage in activities throughout the day. St Mark's is raising money to build a two-storey centre for an autistic charity serving the whole of Bedfordshire, and has recently opened a new community centre offering a suite of light and spacious meeting rooms and a kitchen. This was largely funded by a landfill grant from WREN (Waste Recycling Environmental).

Currently over 45 voluntary and charitable groups use the centre on a regular basis, with over 150 volunteers engaged in helping with projects. More than 300 children under 11 use the building each week and 92 young people are involved in youth groups each week. In total nearly 1,500 people come to the Centre every week. The Centre is home to the parish council whose meetings take place regularly. The Parish Clerk uses the centre for meeting with members of the community.

The Church, mostly a 1970s building, is also the base for three police and community officers who are housed in an attached room with a small kitchen which can easily be reached from outside the church. The 'regular' police station is two miles away in Bedford. These officers patrol the area and hold two surgeries a week in the Church foyer. People come to report petty crimes of vandalism and local nuisance. One of the church leadership team commented: 'it's all part of the community outreach of St Mark's. The church and its hall are in constant use by hundreds of different community organizations.' The Church has set up a website to help other churches wishing to access external funding.

xii. St Michael, Ramsey with Little Oakley, Essex

The village of Ramsey, which has a significant amount of council and social housing, including a development of temporary accommodation for homeless families, was included within the Tendring Rural Development Area, an area so designated on account of social and economic deprivation. At a cost of £101,500 an extension was added to the parish church, a Grade I listed building, to provide a meeting room, kitchen and disabled toilet facilities. This has enabled the church to house a playgroup and a counselling centre and to provide a place for elderly people to get together, space for local committees to meet and a drop-in facility run by Home-Start.

After operating very successfully for two years the counselling service lost its funding and had to close. Four residential homes for the elderly now use the room on a regular basis, with people from the village helping. A Sunday lunch is offered every two months, which is very popular with people living on their own for whom Sunday is 'the loneliest day'. There is also a 'village lunch' every two months on a weekday which attracts other people. The school uses the church for project work now that toilet facilities are available. A youth group has started and members have given concerts in church and taken the occasional evening service. The room is used for courses and discussion groups. The church believes that the project has made a tremendous impact on the community, and the work with elderly people from the residential homes has attracted volunteers who are not church members.

xiii. Denton Chapel

Denton chapel, a 17th-century building shared by URC and Anglican congregations, occupies a central point in the village, which is near Bungay in Suffolk. The Anglicans worship alternately at the parish church and at the chapel. Both church and chapel provide venues for activities such as concerts and exhibitions and the chapel vestry becomes a Post Office each Thursday morning, thus allowing villagers to draw their pensions and carry out any other postal business without having to journey to the next town. Coffee is served on this morning by volunteers who encourage people to stay and catch up on news.

xiv. Towards a Cultural Strategy for Churches in the East Midlands

A survey of 250 churches commissioned by the East Midlands Churches Forum and published in June 2004 found that on average churches run nine activities per week, usually including activities for pre-schoolers and parents, children's activities, activities in local schools, social groups and music groups. Church activity for under-18s was found to benefit a majority of non-church members. Churches responding to the survey were found to contribute more than the equivalent to £1.4 million per year in church-run and individual community activities (if the hourly rate is taken as the average wage for Derbyshire in the year the data was collected). If extrapolated across all churches in Derbyshire, it was estimated that contribution would be worth over £5 million.

xv. St Philip's Centre for Study and Engagement in a Multi-faith Society, Leicester

The St Philip's Centre is located in the refurbished St Philip's Church in the heart of a thriving Muslim, Sikh and Hindu area of Leicester. It has been designated as one of two national centres for training those who minister in multi-faith areas, and preparing secular agencies for work in such areas. St Philip's Church built up a strong inter-faith work over ten years, and the Centre now provides a focus for evening classes, day workshops and longer residential courses aimed at fostering inter-faith dialogue and facilitating education and training for Christian ministers and for those of other faiths and civic partners. It enables Christians and churches to be a confident presence in a multi-faith world prepared to share their own faith and learn from others. The Centre encourages participants to reflect on the implications of a multi-faith from the perspective of issues such as asylum-seeking, family life, education and young people. It also provides training for leaders from voluntary and statutory agencies keen to know more about the role of faith-based organisations. Most of the courses take place in the refurbished St Philip's Church, which was built to seat 600 and has been adapted to create a flexible space including several syndicated rooms. It is still a place of worship and also continues to be used for community events. Two play groups use the church, as does the local council for various events.

xvi. All Saints, Sheepy Magna, Leicestershire

The village post office in Sheepy Magna in Leicester closed in 2003 leaving a vacuum in the village where many people are elderly and without transport. The village shop had also closed earlier. The post office authorities were looking for a replacement and the local vicar offered her church, All Saints, as a replacement. Post Office, borough council and church authorities approved the plans and twelve modest grants were obtained to set up a sub-post office in the base of the tower, together with disabled toilet, a community help desk and a tea and coffee area. This move saved not only the post office but the church's 16th-century tower. The post office opens two mornings a week and is used by 40-50 people per week. The community help desk, which offers advice on everything from planning permission to recycling, is staffed by the borough council and is to be further strengthened by a pensions advice service. Locally baked bread and confectionery products are now sold on post office days and a carers' support help desk is provided once a month by the Borough Voluntary Service Office. A Care and Repair Home Scheme is also run during October for pensioners and the council has set up a CONNECT computer point in the church so that people can easily access county hall services when the church is open.

xvii. St Michael and All Angels, Stanton-by-Dale, Diocese of Derby

Following the closure of the village post office in 1988, the church won a bid to run this service in a converted air-raid shelter on land which it owned. A member of the congregation became sub-postmistress and the post office re-opened in December 1989. In January 1990 it began to sell groceries and greengroceries. The church has subsidised the venture and a church limited company with two nominal directors operates it. The provision of good parking space and accessible entrance makes the shop and post office attractive to less mobile local residents who would previously have struggled to park and get around in the nearby towns. The growth of the service has led to the design and construction of a new post office and shop, a one-storey building which houses a mini supermarket, selling much local produce, and a small coffee area. The Church Community Fund gave £5,000 to help the church build these new premises. The vicar comments that 'it was and still is the church providing a service to the village which it desperately needs. Probably the whole village comes in sometime during a period of two or three weeks and neighbouring ones as well. This is an exciting opportunity for us to build on the excellent relationships between the church and community.'

xviii. Three Churches in Byker, Newcastle

St Silas, which found itself at the centre of a regeneration project with the houses which once surrounded it all gone, is now home to the Byker Bridge Housing Association. The nave has become a well-used community space, and the chancel is retained for worship.

With the aid of SureStart money, St Martin's church was demolished and a new church incorporating a nursery and community space for up to 20 organisations. Flexible spaces mean that the building can be used for a variety of purposes.

St Michael's, a Grade II listed building which was the original parish church of Byker, is at the centre of a project called Aspire, a community partnership working out how best to use this building for the future of that part of Newcastle. The church occupies a distinctive site in the heart of the Byker estate, and the Parochial Church Council has been seeking to re-develop the church site in line with the wishes of the local community and reflecting the themes of arts, heritage and culture.

These developments are not stand-alone projects but have developed out of an Urban Ministry and Theology project set up by the churches to explore their role in Byker and how they should relate to regeneration.

xix. St Mary the Virgin, Stannington, Newcastle Diocese

St Mary's was looking for ways to become more involved in the community at a time when the local council was looking for a centre to provide free access to computers and IT tuition for local residents. The two came together and now, following refurbishment, six computers are installed in the tower room and the IT suite is open one day a week for whoever wants to use it. Most using the suite are pensioners, some of whom have never touched a computer before. The borough provides one tutor and members of the congregation also help out. As demand grows, the number of days the centre is open will increase. The vicar says that the suite is giving the church a higher profile in the village and that the age range of the congregation is beginning to change, with more families attending, enough for them soon to start a regular family service each month.

xx. 'Angels and Advocates: Church Social Action in Yorkshire and the Humber'

According to this report the 4,000 churches and 420,000 active Christians in Yorkshire and the Humber engage in some 6,500 social action projects. Between 50,000 and 70,000 churchgoers are regularly involved in church social action and a similar number engage in social action not organised by the churches. There are some 3,000 staff on church projects from which over 150,000 people benefit. The economic value of church social action to the region is likely to be between £55 and £75 million a year.

xxi. Churches and Neighbourhood Action (CANA)

CANA was set up in 1986 by Barnardo's partly in response to issues raised by the *Faith in the City* report. At the heart of this project is a recognition that churches can play a major role in supporting local communities to respond positively to issues affecting them. CANA works in the urban areas of West Yorkshire and often uses cultural activity such as sports as a vehicle for positive action. CANA works with the Churches Regional Commission and the West Yorkshire African Caribbean Council of Churches to develop an intergenerational oral history project involving five Black Majority Churches in Bradford

xxii. St John's Bowling Parish Church Youth and Drug Dependency Project, Bradford.

East Bowling is an area of multiple deprivation. The community is multi-ethnic. Over 27% of the population is under 16 years of age (higher than the district average) and almost 20% of children live in lone parent families. The Youth Base project grew from street work with young people in the early 1990s'. It is an outreach project operating under the umbrella of Olive Branch Trust, a registered charity of which the vicar of St John's is Chair of the Trustees. Employing seven people as well as volunteers, it is the only youth provision of its kind in East Bowling and offers formal education in an informal setting, study support, careers guidance, support and advice, other resources and activities such as street hockey, and break dancing. There are closed sessions for girls to allow the Asian Community to take part. A former factory unit purchased last year for £238,000 is now the base for a project to help young people who have a drug problem. Supporters and partners of Youth Base include Holmewood Advice Centre, West Yorkshire Police, Careers Bradford, Bradford Metropolitan Council Recreation Division, Bradford Cathedral Community College, Aids Care and Education and Training, Youth Justice, Local Authority.

xxiii. Responding to Flooding: St Michael's, Hull, Diocese of York

When the residents of Orchard Park, Hull, suffered flood damage in 2007 everybody's washing machine was ruined. Though St Michael's stayed dry its laundry equipment broke down, but with donations from various voluntary organisations a brand new industrial-sized washing machine was installed in the church hall and the tumble drier was repaired. The Mothers' Union provided enough washing powder for 1168 washes so members of the community living in their bedrooms or in caravans were able to book time to do their washing and get a cup of tea in return for a small donation.

xxiv. Holy Trinity, North Ormesby

North Ormesby is an urban priority area in Middlesbrough (within the 2% of most deprived wards in England). The old church hall had been serving the community since 1894, but was structurally failing. The parish decided to build a new multi-purpose church-owned and run community centre linked to the Grade II church and facing the market place. An appeal was launched and in eight months one of England's most needy communities had raised over £800,000. Money came from 29 regional and local organisations and trusts including The Community Fund, and the Middlesbrough Partnership through the Neighbourhood Renewal Fund, the Middlesbrough Single Regeneration Budget, Lloyds TSB, English Partnerships, The Diocese of York Social Care Fund, Dow Chemical Company and not least the 1st North Ormesby Baden-Powell Scouts and the North Ormesby Minstrels. The Trinity Centre now offers its local community a 200-seater main hall capable of sub-division; a flexible stage for performances; meeting rooms and offices of various sizes; modern well-equipped kitchen facilities; a link with the main church and cloistered garden. The Centre is now used for coffee mornings, bingo, scouts, after-school clubs, a project which brings performing arts to children, drama and dance groups, suicide care, teenage contraceptive advice, health facilities, slimming clubs, flower club, Jazz Band and a Monday Club for over 60's. The Primary Care Trust and many local children's groups also use the centre.

Seen as the flagship for regeneration of the area, partnerships have been formed with the University of Teesside School of Health and Social Care, and the Middlesbrough Primary Care Trust to provide training and advice to the community. As further evidence of the confidence that this project has now brought to the area, Tees Valley Housing is developing £5m of new social housing next to the Centre and is keen to see the Centre offering a service to local residents. There is also to be a £7m new medical village. The former archbishop of York commented that 'The Trinity Centre, centre by name and central by location, offers a new and exciting possibility for both Church and community in North Ormesby. I believe it is a clear sign that the Church's place is always right at the heart of the community it seeks to serve.'

xxv. Campitor Ltd based at St Catherine's Church, Sandal Magna, Wakefield

Campitor aims to facilitate cohesion and help young people bridge the gap between the different cultures and lifestyles that exist within the parish. It provides day care for elderly people under a contract with the local authority; transport, catering and employment-support enterprises; and runs a community-research company and management training consultancy. The project is run by the community and although very much aligned with the Church of England's charitable objectives, it is 'careful' to separate the church's function from its own. A £0.3m European Development Fund grant has been awarded to develop Campitor further.

The vicar says that the church 'is not looking for a cash return, but to be socially or ethically beneficial. We are operating in a market of values, trading in positive values about and for society. It is motivated by values and commitments found in Christianity in terms of community well-being and the relief of poverty.' He says that the church has benefited from the project: when he was installed in the early 1990s the church was disengaged from the neighbourhood and community. 'Only 10% of the parish knew where it was and there were only two children and a couple of dozen elderly people. Now there is a new church centre, including conference and training facilities and on Sundays up to 70-80 adults and 20-30 children.'

APPENDIX E

Timeline of Faith Founded or Church Incubated Organisations/Projects

1940: Progressio

1949: Christian Aid

1956: Defence And Aid Fund (now the Canon Collins Educational Trust for Southern Africa) launched to provide legal aid funding for those being trialled for 'treason' and then political reasons in South Africa. 1956 to 1991 the Fund sent £100 million in defence of thousands of political activists and provide for their families while they were in prison. The trust largely funded the defence costs of the Rivonia Triallists – including Nelson Mandela – on whose legal team was Lord Joel Joffe.

1958: The Academy of St Martin in the Fields was formed in 1958 as a small, conductorless chamber ensemble. Led by Neville Marriner and attracting some of the finest players in London, the orchestra at first concentrated on repertoire from the Baroque era, developing a style of performance that launched the 1960's Baroque revival. The Academy was so named after the various concert-giving societies or 'Academies' that had flourished in 18th century London and the famous church in which it gave its first concert on 13 November 1959.

1962: CAFOD

1963: The Simon Community was founded by Anton Wallich-Clifford in 1963 and is a registered charity (no. 283938). Anton's vision for Simon was to reach out to the homeless and rootless, to be a movement of concern and, by working as a community, to offer a radical alternative to institutional care.

1969: Centrepoint: In the winter, Ken Leech, and the Simon Community became so concerned about the young people sleeping on the streets in the West End that they decided to do something about it. He and a group of volunteers from the Simon Community opened the basement of his church, St Anne's in Soho, on the 16th December as a temporary night shelter.

1974: Richard Adams founded Tearcraft which was one of the earliest fair trade social enterprises and was backed by TEAR Fund. Adams was a student at St John's College with Cranmer Hall in Durham and chair of the Student Christian Movement from 1994-7. In 2005-06 he was New Statesman social entrepreneur of the year.

1979: Traidcraft plc was also founded by Richard Adams and has grown today into a major social enterprise with stakes in Twin Trading and Café Direct. It has five principal aims: to tackle poverty by creating a market for the fair trade producers to supply; to demonstrate to other organisations that it is possible to run a commercially viable company using fair trade principles; to provide learning opportunities for Traidcraft as a whole, by giving greater substance and credibility to the advocacy and campaigning work; to educate consumers of the benefit of fair trade purchases so they will put pressure on other organisations and the government to adopt fairer trade rules; to provide the choice to consumers who are looking to make a moral decision on goods that they purchase.

1985: Bromley By Bow Centre

1986: The Kaleidoscope needle exchange in South London began operating in September 1986 as part of a wider church-based project which was also involved in methadone prescription and other, non drug-related social problems. The project was established in purpose-built accommodation and was unusual for UK schemes in that it was open seven days a week from 7am to 11pm and remained open all night on Fridays. The Kaleidoscope Project is a church-based community project established over 30 years ago by the Rev Eric Blakebrough MBE and the members of the John Bunyan Baptist Church in Kingston. Eric Blakeborough is named as the most influential figure in the development of Andrew Mawson's social entrepreneurship and is the father of Rev Adele Blakeborough who has gone on to found the ICAN (community action network) network and its social enterprise hub on London's South Bank

1988: FRC Group in Liverpool. Founded by Rev Nic Frances with support from the Diocese of Liverpool. Having built FRC up and been awarded an MBE for his work he moved to his native Melbourne where he became Executive Director of the Brotherhood of St Laurence and Chair of the Australian social enterprise network. Its subsequent Chief Executive was Liam Black who had cut his teeth in the sector working for the Archdiocese of Liverpool Justice and Peace Commission. FRC is a leading social enterprise in the UK. Black went on to be Chief Executive of Jamie Oliver's Fifteen Foundation rolling out its social restaurant concept to the UK regions and mainland Europe.

2004: Campitor St Catherine: Founded from St Catherine's Church, Wakefield in 2004 by drawing together a range of initiatives developed over a 15 year period, the Campitor St Catherine Co-operative is a community-owned social enterprise with a proven track record of supporting individuals in terms of their education, skills and employability; delivering services that contribute to the well-being of neighbourhoods and communities such as training, education, research, community transport; providing a mechanism for sustainable initiatives in which local communities have a real ownership stake

APPENDIX F

Dissemination

This report has been focused on particular aspects of public service reform, community participation and the faith communities. As previously stated, it is based on an exploratory enquiry for one particular Christian denomination. As such it forms one part of an ongoing conversation in academic and policy-making communities on the one hand and within the various religious traditions in the UK on the other. At this stage the following activities are confirmed to extend this process of conversation more broadly.

Faith Community:
2008

- 13 May: William Temple 60th anniversary lecture/ Ronald Preston Memorial Lecture - University of Manchester
- 17 June: Urban Bishops
- 19 June: North West Bishops
- 4-8 July: General Synod (York)

- September: Catholic Union – South of England Day Conference

Academic Community - Religious

2008

- October: A special edition of the *International Journal of Public Theology*, guest edited by Francis Davis and Andrew Bradstock and themed around 'Theology, Well Being and Welfare'

2009

- October: A special edition of the journal *Political Theology* on 'Theology, Public Policy And Welfare Reform', guest edited by Francis Davis and Elizabeth Paulhus.

- December: A special edition of the journal *Crucible* on 'Community, Civic participation and Renewal – Faith based insights', guest edited by Francis Davis and Elizabeth Paulhus.

Academic Community – Social Sciences

2009

- October: Special edition Journal of *Public Money and Management* (Blackwells), guest edited by Francis Davis, Elizabeth Paulhus and George Wilkes

- December: 'Case Studies in Faith-based Community Action' Blackfriars Hall/Von Hügel Institute by Francis Davis

Central and Local Government/Voluntary Sector and the Regions:

2008

- June: Lancashire Launch hosted by William Hampson DL, Deputy Lieutenant for Greater Manchester and Freeman, Wigan Borough.

- September: A Regional Conversation on Faith, Civil Society and Policy, organised by Oxford Diocesan Board for Social Responsibility and hosted by Rt Rev John Pritchard, Bishop of Oxford.

- Autumn: University of Cambridge Institute for Continuing Education/ Von Hügel Institute Seminar on 'Religion And Public Policy' jointly with the Public Management and Policy Association

Further Studies:

An Assessment of the Christian Value Added of the YMCA in Norwich and the Civic Contribution of the Faith Communities in Norwich – to include reference group of the Bishop of Norwich and Rt Hon Stephen Timms MP